Mac OS X Lion
Pocket Guide

Chris Seibold

Beijing · Cambridge · Farnham · Köln · Sebastopol · Tokyo

Mac OS X Lion Pocket Guide
by Chris Seibold

Copyright © 2011 Chris Seibold. All rights reserved.
Printed in Canada.

Published by O'Reilly Media, Inc., 1005 Gravenstein Highway North, Sebastopol, CA 95472.

O'Reilly books may be purchased for educational, business, or sales promotional use. Online editions are also available for most titles (*http://my.safari booksonline.com*). For more information, contact our corporate/institutional sales department: (800) 998-9938 or *corporate@oreilly.com*.

Editor: Dawn Mann
Production Editor: Teresa Elsey
Proofreader: Teresa Elsey
Indexer: Newgen North America, Inc.
Cover Designer: Karen Montgomery
Interior Designer: David Futato
Illustrator: Robert Romano

Printing History:
August 2011:   First Edition.

ISBN: 978-1-449-31058-5

[TM]

1312549985

Contents

Preface

OS X was first released to the public over a decade ago as Mac OS X Beta (code-named Kodiak). The decade after that introduction saw Mac OS X go from an interesting oddity unsuited to daily work to a usable operating system (OS) with little third-party support to everything most people want out of an operating system and a little more.

Lion is the latest version of OS X, and it offers a stunning number of new features. It includes changes as seemingly mundane as resizing windows from any edge and those as revolutionary as installing Lion without using physical media.

Like your iPhone? Love your iPad? Then you're going to really enjoy Lion. Many features in Lion were first found in iOS, the operating system that powers the iPhone and iPad. You'll discover Launchpad, a method of opening applications very similar to the way you do on an iPhone. And the similarities don't stop with launching applications: Launchpad also lets you create folders by dragging apps on top of each other, just as you can on your iOS device.

But there's a lot more to Lion than just some iOS-inspired features. Many applications have new features or, as in the case of Mail, received a complete overhaul of the interface and design. You'll also be treated to the immersive experience of a bevy of full-screen applications.

The geeky side of Mac users hasn't been forgotten, either. There's a new full-screen version of Terminal, better security options, and the ability to remotely control another Mac in full-screen so it feels exactly like you're sitting in front of the far-away Mac.

You'll also be relieved to know that the cost of all the improvements and new features that comprise Lion is unchanged from the price of Snow Leopard: $29. Better yet, you don't have to leave your Mac to get it. Instead of hitting the Apple Store and picking up a DVD or waiting for a copy to be shipped to you, you can get Lion directly from the Mac App Store. Yup, Apple's most ambitious OS upgrade since Mac OS changed to OS X is just a download away.

NOTE

This book focuses on what you'd see on screen if you bought a brand-new Mac with Lion on it. If you upgrade from Snow Leopard to Lion, some things you see may be slightly different, because some settings will get transferred over from Snow Leopard. This book tries to point out such instances whenever applicable, but you may spot differences not noted here.

Conventions Used in This Book

This book uses the following typographical conventions:

Italic

> Indicates new terms, URLs, email addresses, filenames, and file extensions.

`Constant width bold`

> Shows commands or other text that should be typed literally by the user.

`Constant width italic`

> Shows text that should be replaced with user-supplied values or by values determined by context.

Menu Symbols

With this Pocket Guide, you'll always know which button to press. The key labeled "option" is called Option throughout this book. The key with the clover symbol (officially called the Place of Interest symbol) is represented by ⌘, which looks precisely like the symbol on the keyboard.

Apple itself uses some symbols for these keys that you won't see on your keyboard. If you click the menu bar, you'll see symbols next to some commands that indicate their keyboard shortcuts. For example, if you click the Edit menu while running TextEdit, you'll see a long sequence of symbols for the "Paste and Match Style" shortcut, as shown in Figure P-1.

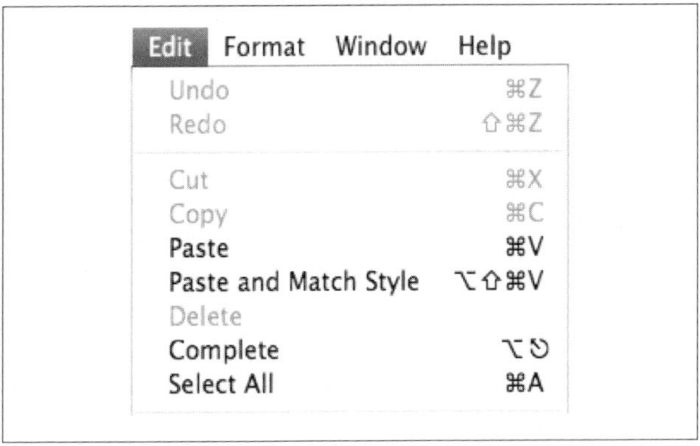

Edit	Format	Window	Help
Undo			⌘Z
Redo			⇧⌘Z
Cut			⌘X
Copy			⌘C
Paste			⌘V
Paste and Match Style			⌥⇧⌘V
Delete			
Complete			⌥↺
Select All			⌘A

Figure P-1. Keyboard shortcuts in TextEdit's Edit menu

From left to right, the symbols to the right of "Paste and Match Style" are Option (⌥), Shift (⇧), and Command (the ⌘ described earlier). This indicates that you need to hold down the Option, Shift, and ⌘ keys while pressing V. In this book, you'll see this written as "Option-Shift-⌘-V" instead.

A less commonly used modifier is the Control key, which Apple indicates with the ⌃ symbol. This book spells it out as "Control." You may also encounter ⎋, which indicates the Esc key.

The symbol for the Eject button (⏏) is the same as the symbol that is silk-screened onto most Apple keyboards. The Delete key is symbolized with ⌫.

Attribution and Permissions

This book is here to help you get your job done. If you reference limited parts of it in your work or writings, we appreciate, but don't require, attribution. An attribution usually includes the title, author, publisher, and ISBN, like so: "*Mac OS X Lion Pocket Guide*, by Chris Seibold (O'Reilly). Copyright 2011 Chris Seibold, 978-1-449-31058-5."

If you feel your use of examples or quotations from this book falls outside fair use or the permission given above, feel free to contact us at *permissions@oreilly.com*.

Safari® Books Online

Safari Safari Books Online is an on-demand digital library that lets you easily search over 7,500 technology and creative reference books and videos to find the answers you need quickly.

With a subscription, you can read any page and watch any video from our library online. Read books on your cell phone and mobile devices. Access new titles before they are available for print, and get exclusive access to manuscripts in development and post feedback for the authors. Copy and paste code samples, organize your favorites, download chapters, bookmark key sections, create notes, print out pages, and benefit from tons of other time-saving features.

O'Reilly Media has uploaded this book to the Safari Books Online service. To have full digital access to this book and others on similar topics from O'Reilly and other publishers, sign up for free at *http://my.safaribooksonline.com*.

How to Contact Us

Please address comments and questions concerning this book to the publisher:

O'Reilly Media, Inc.
1005 Gravenstein Highway North
Sebastopol, CA 95472
800-998-9938 (in the United States or Canada)
707-829-0515 (international or local)
707-829-0104 (fax)

We have a web page for this book, where we list errata, examples, and any additional information. You can access this page at:

http://www.oreilly.com/catalog/9781449310585

To comment or ask technical questions about this book, send email to:

bookquestions@oreilly.com

For more information about our books, courses, conferences, and news, see our website at *http://www.oreilly.com*.

Find us on Facebook: *http://facebook.com/oreilly*

Follow us on Twitter: *http://twitter.com/oreillymedia*

Watch us on YouTube: *http://www.youtube.com/oreillymedia*

Acknowledgments

I'd like to thank Dawn Mann for turning this into a readable book, and Bakari Chavanu for making sure the tech stuff was correct. Thanks to Brian Jepson for teaching me so much and Hadley Stern for getting me involved in writing books. And finally, thanks to Yen Hong for watching Nathaniel while I was banging away at the keyboard.

CHAPTER 1

What's New in Lion?

Surely there are some people who pine for the days of the Apple II and the command-line interface. For those who have moved on from the era of loading programs from cassette tapes and floppy disks, Lion is the latest version of Apple's OS X, and it's a large step forward from Snow Leopard, which came out in 2009. If you ask someone what has changed with Lion, they might tell you "Just about everything," and they'd be right. But don't let the changes in Lion scare you—even though differences abound, if you want to keep using your Mac the same way you used it with an earlier version of OS X, you'll still be able to use Lion without any problems.

Once you've used Lion for a few minutes, you'll note that a lot of the features that you find different in Lion seem a lot like IOS, the operating system that powers your iPhone and iPad. Lion isn't a naked copy of iOS—what works in a finger-driven OS doesn't always work in a keyboard- and mouse-driven environment—but the success of the iOS devices has clearly had an impact on the Mac side of Apple. Like the iPhone and iPad, Lion gives you access to an App Store (devoted to Macs). You also get the option of using a screen similar to iOS for launching applications, and Mail has become a lot more like the iPhone Mail app.

Those are just a few obvious changes, but there are plenty more. As you'd expect, many of the applications and utilities that get installed along with OS X have been updated for Lion's coming-out party. There are too many enhancements to list quickly, so the rest of this chapter focuses on the major differences between Lion and previous versions of OS X. See Chapter 6 to learn about changes to specific applications, and Chapter 3 to find out about changes specific the Finder and how you control OS X. For now, it's time to see what all the fuss is about!

Getting Your Hands on Lion

The first big difference you'll notice between Lion and previous versions of OS X is how you acquire a copy. Instead of waiting for a DVD in the mail or heading down to your local Apple Store to buy it, you download Lion straight from the Mac App Store. Apple calls this "electronic distribution," but it amounts to a more convenient way of getting Lion onto your Mac. For info on downloading and installing Lion, see Chapter 2.

NOTE

Actually, you have a couple of other ways of getting Lion, though downloading it is the cheapest and fastest method (assuming you have a good Internet connection). To learn about your other options, check out the Note under "Installing Lion" on page 22.

The lack of physical installation media might be disturbing to some. What if you have problems and need to reinstall the OS? What if your hard drive needs repair? With no physical media, how can you start your Mac from a separate disk? Happily, Apple provides a solution to all those problems. When you install Lion, you also install an emergency startup disk that you can use to reinstall Lion, launch the utilities found in OS X to try to repair any problems you're having, and browse the Internet to look for a solution. (If you find yourself in a tough spot, see Chapter 4 for some basic Lion troubleshooting techniques.)

And there's even better news about getting Lion from the Mac App Store: you can install it on any authorized Mac that meets the hardware requirements! That means you can forget about paying for the family pack—paying for Lion once lets you install it on up to five Macs.

A Brand-New Look

Snow Leopard looked a lot like Leopard, which looked a lot like Tiger. Each major revision of OS X brought some visual changes, but they tended to not be all that noticeable. The look of Lion is the most ambitious change in appearance since Apple went from OS 9 to OS X. When you see Lion in action, you'll still recognize it as OS X, but you're liable to imagine you're looking at some futuristic version of OS X available five years from now instead of the current version. A picture's worth a thousand words, so check out Figures 1-1 and 1-2.

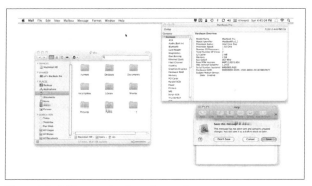

Figure 1-1. A Mac running Snow Leopard

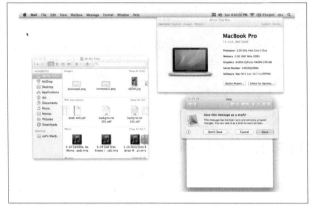

Figure 1-2. The new look of Lion

Some things jump out at you right away: The buttons look different and you seemingly can't scroll around in a page anymore, because the scroll bars are gone. Actually, the scroll bars are still around, but they only show up when you need them (if you don't like this behavior, you can change it; see Chapter 5).

Those are the most obvious visual differences, but you'll find other changes as you acquaint yourself with Lion. Don't be overly concerned with the differences—as new as everything looks, if you've used a previous version of OS X, you'll be able to get around in Lion with minimal effort.

Resize from Any Edge

In previous versions of OS X, windows usually had resize handles in their lower-right corners. In Lion, those handles are gone and you can change a window's size from any edge. To pull this trick off, hover your cursor over the edge of a window and the cursor will change to a double-headed arrow; simply drag to resize the window.

If you're used to moving windows by grabbing an edge and dragging, that won't work in Lion—you'll simply resize the window. You'll have to adjust your habits and click inside the window to drag it.

Full-Screen Applications

Ever longed for a more immersive Web-browsing experience, or wished that iCal would take over every pixel of screen space? At first, such longings may sound silly, but having Safari fill your screen when you're reading a longish Wikipedia entry is great, and working in iCal using the entire screen is fantastic when you are using its new heat map feature (see the section on "iCal" on page 164).

Not every application has a Full Screen mode, but it's easy to figure out which ones can suck up all your screen real estate: look for the double arrows in the upper-right corner of the program's window (Figure 1-3).

Figure 1-3. Clicking the double arrows tells the app to take over your screen

Once the application is in Full Screen mode, you can do whatever you wish, free from the distractions of your desktop and other programs. When you're using that application, move your cursor to the top of the screen and the menu bar will reappear. Click the blue arrows on the right end of the menu bar to return the program to a regular window.

You may be thinking that full-screen applications *seem* like a great idea, but that they might be a little too much work when you need to use another program or get back to the desktop. Don't worry, there are plenty of easy ways to get out of a full-screen application. You can switch programs with the Option-Tab key combo, hit the Esc key to exit Full Screen mode, or invoke the new and very cool Mission Control.

NOTE

If you use multiple monitors, you might be hoping for a world where you can run one application in Full Screen mode while doing something else on the other monitor. Sadly, you're out of luck: launching a full-screen application in Lion renders the second monitor useless—unless your goal is to look at a static, gray linen screen.

Mission Control

Mission Control replaces Exposé, and you're going to love it. In a nutshell, Mission Control is a window-management application. But that description, while accurate, is far too terse. OS X Lion features Spaces (virtual desktops for your different workflow needs; "Spaces" on page 98 has details), Dashboard for the information that you want quick access to (see "The Dashboard" on page 87), full-screen applications, and the regular windowed applications you know and love. That's four distinctly different ways of interacting with your Mac.

Switching between a full-screen application and the desktop would be cumbersome. Mission Control takes care of that: instead of forcing you to click and hunt for minimized windows, Mission Control puts everything going on on your Mac into one easy-to-navigate window. For example, if you happen to be writing a book, launching Mission Control might reveal a monitor that looks like Figure 1-4.

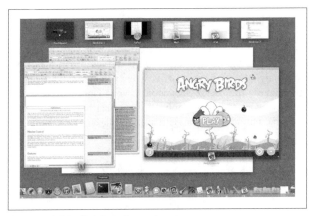

Figure 1-4. It's all right in front of you!

You use Mission Control by either pressing F3 (on most keyboards) or swiping up with three fingers on your trackpad (you can adjust this in the Mission Control preference pane; see "Mission Control" on page 122). When you invoke Mission Control, you see Dashboard, your desktop, Spaces, and any open full-screen apps across the top. Normal application windows appear in the center of the screen (grouped by application), and the Dock is wherever you left it.

Once Mission Control is active, you can add desktop spaces by dragging a window to the upper-right corner of your screen (a + sign will appear). If you want to add an empty desktop space, move your cursor to that same corner and click the +. To delete a space, put your cursor over it and click the × that appears.

Once you decide where you want to go (that pesky game of Angry Birds or the book you're writing, say), just click the window you want to jump to. Swipes also work if you're using a trackpad: a quick swipe to the left or right will switch between applications.

Launchpad

Got an iOS device? If so, Launchpad will seem very familiar; it behaves just like the screen on your iPhone or iPad. For the uninitiated, here's how it works: when you launch Launchpad (by clicking the rocket ship icon in your Dock), your screen fades away and all your applications appear in icon form (Figure 1-5). Launch any one with a single click.

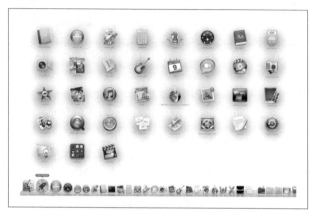

Figure 1-5. It's like you're staring at a giant iPhone

If the only thing you have installed on your Mac is Lion, all your applications' icons will fit on a single screen. If you've added applications, you'll need more than a single screen to hold them all. Navigating between screens is easy: just two-finger swipe left or right on the trackpad or with a capable mouse to move from page to page.

The application icons are grouped automatically. If you aren't happy with the results, just click an icon, hold your mouse button until all the icons start wiggling, and then drag the icon where you want it to live. (Click any empty spot on the screen to make the icons stop wiggling.) Too many pages of icons? You can create folders in Launchpad. Simply drag one icon on top of another and Launchpad creates a folder containing those applications and gives it a name (Figure 1-6). If Lion chooses a poor name for your folder or you just want a snappier one, click the folder to open it and then click the name of the folder. Lion will highlight the name and you'll be able to change it to one of your choosing. To delete a folder, open it and then drag the program icons out of it; once there's only a single icon in the folder, the folder disappears.

Figure 1-6. A folder in Launchpad

NOTE

Any folders you create and any application reordering you do in Launchpad is only reflected in Launchpad; the folders and applications remain in the same place you left them when viewed with the Finder.

Surprisingly, you can banish applications from your Mac with Launchpad, though only ones you've purchased from the Mac App Store. To delete applications with Launchpad, press and hold the Option key so all the icons start jiggling. Icons for applications you can delete will have a white × in their top-left corners. Click the × and you'll be warned about deleting the application; confirm your choice and the program is gone. (Deleting an application isn't as permanent as it sounds: since you purchased it from the Mac App Store, you can download it again for free if you ever want it back.)

All My Files

There are a ton of files running around your Mac, but you probably don't care about the random ones like *image-viewport.html*—you care about the files *you've* created. All My Files filters out all the clutter and lets you get to the important files on your Mac.

When you click All My Files in the Finder's sidebar, you're presented with (you guessed it) all your files (Figure 1-7). That doesn't sound too exciting, but it is.

Figure 1-7. The most useful item in the sidebar

Your files will be grouped by type and you can reorder them as you wish. You can quickly sort through your files using a variety of criteria (date modified, size, etc.) and find exactly what you want. Once you've used All My Files a few times, you'll wonder how you ever got along without it.

Gestures

To make getting around your Mac easier, Apple has added new gestures. Gestures are fairly intuitive multifinger swipes, pinches, and taps that make jumping from desktop space to space (to cite one example) much easier. You can use gestures with a Magic Mouse or trackpad, though the gestures for each device differ and you get many more options with a trackpad. For a complete list of gestures, see "Multitouch trackpads" on page 139.

AirDrop

The good news: Lion features a brand-new, very easy, zero-configuration way to transfer files between Macs; it's called AirDrop. The bad news: if your Mac is more than a few years old, this method probably won't work.

How can you tell whether your Mac can use AirDrop? Simply open a Finder window; if you see the AirDrop icon in the sidebar (see Figure 1-8), your Mac is AirDrop capable.

Figure 1-8. This Mac is ready for an AirDrop

When you click the AirDrop icon, your Mac starts looking for nearby Macs. When it finds one, just drag the file you want to send onto the icon for that user in the AirDrop window (Figure 1-8). The recipient will get a notice that you want to transfer the file, and, once he grants the request, the file will speedily move to his Mac. It's a slick system that doesn't rely on your WiFi network connection (AirDrop uses the WiFi built into your Mac instead), so you can share files with someone nearby even when you're not connected to a network.

Auto Save and Versions

Two of the coolest new features in Lion are Auto Save and the associated Versions. Auto Save does exactly what its name implies: as you work on a document, song, movie, or whatever, Auto Save automatically saves your progress incrementally so you don't have to. Working in TextEdit and just want to quit? You don't need to save before quitting—Auto Save will save your work without being told to. Versions are the result of all those saves. With Versions, if there's a change you want to undo, you aren't stuck with the most recent version of your file.

We'll use TextEdit as an example. Once you create a document, save it, and then make a change to it, the word "Edited" will appear in the title bar to let you know that Auto Save is working. Click "Edited" to reveal a drop-down menu that gives you four options:

Lock

This option allows you to lock the document. Once it's locked, you won't be able to edit the document, but you can use it as a template for a new document. Think of this as way of being sure you don't make any boneheaded changes to something you worked long and hard to create.

Duplicate

Choosing this option lets you create a copy of either the current version of the file you're working on or the most recent version of it (without your latest changes) that you explicitly saved with the Save command.

Revert to Last Saved Version

This allows you to revert to the last version you explicitly saved with the Save command (not the latest version that Auto Save created).

Browse All Versions

This is where Versions comes in. If you've made some changes to your file that you like and some that you hate, you can use Versions to pick out the moment in time when your file was at its best. Select this option from the drop-down menu and you'll see a screen (shown in Figure 1-9) reminiscent of Time Machine. You can then flip through the incremental changes Lion has been tracking and pick out the version you like the most.

Figure 1-9. Flip through all the saved versions to find the one you want

---

WARNING

Not every application works with Auto Save. Since it's a new feature, developers have to tweak their programs to make them work with Auto Save, so don't depend on Auto Save to back up your work unless you're *sure* the program you're using supports it.

Resume

When you use an app on an iOS device, the app starts up right where you left off the last time you ran it. Lion has this feature as well: if you quit Safari with ten windows open, those same windows will pop open when you restart Safari. Resume also works when you shut down or log out: do either of those things and, when you restart or log back in, all the apps you were using automatically relaunch and open all the windows you had open before.

This is a nice feature, but it can also be something you don't want. Luckily, you can turn Resume off. Head to System Preferences→General, and then uncheck the box next to "Restore windows when quitting and re-opening apps." This will stop Lion from opening windows when you launch an application, but it won't affect how Resume works when you restart your machine. To turn Resume off when you log out or restart, uncheck the box next to "Reopen windows when logging back in."

Mail

A lot of applications have been updated in Lion; the most extensive changes are in Mail. To learn how to set up accounts and do other mundane chores, see "Mail" on page 166. To learn about the big changes in Mail, keep reading.

When you first open Lion's Mail you'll be shocked—it looks nothing like the Mail you've been using. The colorful rounded buttons are gone; they've been replaced by new, less visually intense buttons. And the changes don't stop there— Figure 1-10 shows just how much Mail has changed.

By default, you get a two-column view and the familiar sidebar is nowhere to be found (however, if you upgrade from Snow Leopard, the sidebar will still be there). If you're wondering how you're going to get around without the sidebar (where your mailboxes and folders were formerly stored), don't fret.

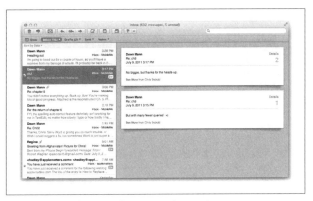

Figure 1-10. Is that even the same application?

You can get the old sidebar back by clicking Show in the brand-new Favorites bar near the top of the window. But chances are you won't want to add the sidebar, as all your mailboxes and folders are also listed in the Favorites bar; just click an item in the bar to navigate to your destination. And you aren't limited to the folders built into the Favorites bar; you can add any folder to the bar by dragging it there from the sidebar.

Messages in Mail are now grouped into conversations. That means the tête-à-tête you've got going with someone won't be a long list of discrete messages; instead, every message in it will be grouped together, reducing clutter and streamlining your Mail experience. You'll see a number with a triangle next to it on each conversation; click the arrow to reveal the individual messages, as shown in Figure 1-11.

If you give the new Mail a chance, you'll probably love it. But if you find it intolerable, head to Mail→Preferences→Viewing and turn on "Use classic layout" to switch to a version of Mail that feels a lot more like the old one.

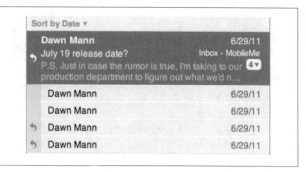

Figure 1-11. A close-up view of Mail's new conversation layout. When you click on a message here, it appears in all its glory on the right side of the Mail window.

What Lion Can't Do

Lion does a lot that previous versions of OS X couldn't, but there are also some things that previous versions did that Lion can't.

Likely your biggest frustration will be programs you have that Lion won't run. The two previous versions of OS X (Leopard and Snow Leopard) could run applications built either for PowerPC-based Macs or Intel-based Macs. Snow Leopard pulled this trick off by using Rosetta, code that dynamically translated PowerPC code into instructions that your Intel-based Mac could use. Lion doesn't include Rosetta, so it won't run any applications except those built with Intel-powered Macs in mind.

If you want to check whether an application will run in Lion before you install Lion, right-click or Control-click the Finder icon of the application in question and select Get Info from the pop-up menu that appears. If you look at the Kind list item and see either "Universal" or "Intel," the app will run in Lion; if you see "PowerPC" instead, forget it. Once you've installed

Lion, it's easy to spot programs that won't run: they'll have big, white No symbols on 'em (Figure 1-12).

RealPlayer

Figure 1-12. Not much of a loss in this case

What else is gone? If you're one of the people who really enjoys the animation that traditionally accompanies a new OS install (you know, the peppy music with "Hello" zipping by in fifty languages), you're in for a disappointment: the opening animation is gone. When Lion gets done installing, it's time to get down to the business of setting up your Mac.

Also missing from the equation is Front Row, but that isn't as a big of a loss as it sounds like. DVD Player can go full screen, so you can get that immersive movie experience when watching DVDs, and sites like Hulu can also take over your entire screen if you wish. iSync is also MIA; one surmises that the demand for this application has dwindled steadily since the introduction of the iPhone and other smartphones. Finally, the Applications folder doesn't appear in the Dock by default (though it will still be there if you upgraded from Snow Leopard). You can always add the Applications folder to your Dock (see "The Dock" on page 72), but Launchpad replicates its functionality nicely.

Aside from the loss of Rosetta, the functionality losses in Lion are minor and are far outweighed by the benefits you get from adopting the latest version of OS X.

CHAPTER 2

Installing Lion and Migrating Data

New Macs come with Lion (10.7) preinstalled, but that doesn't mean buying a new Mac with Lion on it is the only way to get Apple's latest and greatest operating system. A much more economical way to enjoy Lion is to upgrade your current Mac, something you can do for a fraction of the cost of a new machine. This chapter teaches you how.

If you're lucky enough to have a Mac with Lion preinstalled, you likely want to move all or some of the data off your old computer onto your new, Lion-powered Mac. In that case, see "Moving Data and Applications from Another Computer" on page 26 to learn how.

What You Need to Run Lion

Snow Leopard could run on any Intel-based Mac, but Lion is slightly choosier, jettisoning some models of Intel-based Macs from the lineup. To run Lion, you'll need an x86-64 processor or better. If "x86-64" doesn't mean much to you, you're not alone. To help clarify, here are the actual names of chips that meet that criterion:

- Intel Core 2 Duo
- Intel Core i3
- Intel Core i5
- Intel Core i7
- Xeon

Since most people don't bother committing the names of their processors to memory, there's an easy way to find out what kind of chip you have: Go to the Apple menu (🍎) and select About This Mac. The window that appears includes the name of your processor. If it's on the list above, your Mac is compatible.

WARNING

Thanks to a weird naming convention, there's been some confusion over whether certain Macs can run Lion. Ones with Intel Core Duo chips can't run it, but Intel Core 2 Duo chips can.

You also need 2 GB of RAM (which some otherwise compatible MacBooks and Minis might not have) and 5 GB of disk space. If you find checking chip compatibility and memory requirements too tedious, you can opt to let Apple check them instead: launch the Mac App Store and try to purchase Mac OS X Lion; if your Mac comes up short in any department, you won't be allowed to buy it.

In addition to the hardware requirements, your Mac must be running OS X 10.6.7 or later. Why not, say, 10.6.3? Well, you'll be getting Lion from the Mac App Store, and the Mac App Store didn't exist until 10.6.7 was released. If you're running Snow Leopard, just head to 🍎→Software Update. If you're running Leopard, you'll need to find a copy of Snow Leopard and install that before you worry about anything else.

Preparing for the Install

Before deciding whether you actually want Lion, you should do a little detective work. Since Lion won't support PowerPC apps, if you are dependent on one of those for day-to-day work, you'll likely want to avoid Lion or upgrade to new apps before you install Lion. But how do you know?

Luckily, there's a quick way to get at this information in Snow Leopard: Head to →About This Mac, and then click the More Info to display a two-column window. The left column contains a long list of entries that reveal specific information when you select them. Click Applications (in the Software section) and, in the right column, your Mac will tell you about all the apps you have installed. The list is sortable, so if you click Kind (as shown in Figure 2-1), the list will organize the applications into four categories: Intel, Universal, PowerPC, and Classic. If the application you need to have says "PowerPC" next to it, it won't run in Lion. If you don't need any of those clunky PowerPC apps or if you upgrade to later versions of them, you're ready for Lion.

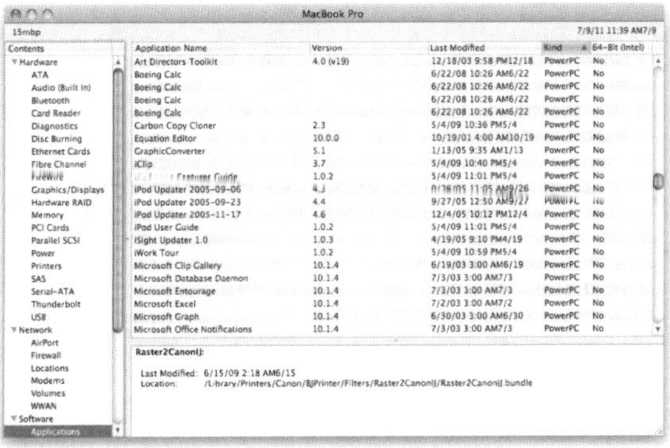

Figure 2-1. None of these will run when you're using Lion

Installing Lion

Before Lion, you had to cram a DVD into your computer to upgrade OS X. With Lion, things have become slightly easier. No more restarting your machine from the comparatively slow DVD; instead, you simply download the installer from the Mac App Store.

NOTE

You don't *have* to download Lion from the Mac App Store. Apple will start selling thumb drives (small memory sticks that plug into a USB port) with the Lion installer on them in August 2011. If you're thinking the thumb drive is a no-brainer, since you get a free drive and all, don't get too excited: it comes at a premium. Instead of paying $29 to download Lion, you pay $69 for the drive. You can order it from *www.store.apple.com*.

Don't want to pay the premium *or* download the installer over a slow Internet connection? Then you can visit an Apple Store and download Lion while you browse all the cool Apple hardware.

Whether you plan on downloading the installer or using a USB thumb drive with the installer on it, the process is dead simple. First, make sure you're running the latest version of Snow Leopard (if not, head to →Software Update). Then, if you're going the download route, open the Mac App Store (click its icon in your Dock), purchase Lion, and wait for it to download. If you're using a thumb drive, plug it into one of the USB slots on your Mac. (If you're just after a physical installer for Lion, the following Note has your solution.)

Once the download is complete or you plug in the thumb drive, the Lion installer should launch automatically. (If it doesn't, you'll likely find an alias for it in your Dock and the original application in your Applications folder if you downloaded it. If you bought a thumb drive, you'll find Lion stored on the drive.) All you have to do to get things really moving is click the Continue button (Figure 2-2).

Once you take the plunge, you'll be presented with a page requiring you to agree to the software license. To install Lion, you'll have to click Agree twice: once in the Install Mac OS X window and once on a drop-down menu that asks if you *really* meant that first click. After that, Lion will toss up a message telling you that it's preparing to install. A few minutes later, you'll be notified that you can either restart your Mac to proceed with the install or wait thirty seconds and let Lion restart for you.

If your Mac operates off of a single drive, the installation will proceed without any input from you. If you have multiple

Figure 2-2. You've got one option: Continue

drives or multiple partitions on a single drive, you'll be able to choose exactly where you want to install Lion.

NOTE

Lion can be installed on any drive (internal or external) that's formatted with Apple's Mac OS Extended (Journaled) filesystem. You can run Disk Utility from the installer's Utilities menu to format or inspect the drives on your system.

After the Install

After Lion is done installing, your Mac will restart using the new operating system. If the Mac has already been configured—that is, if it had an earlier version of Mac OS X installed—you'll be prompted to register your copy of Lion (hit ⌘-Q to skip registration; doing so is no big deal). Additionally, you might see a message that says your mail needs to be upgraded to work with the new version of Mail. Other than that, you can get back to using your Mac just like you did before you installed Lion (with some cool new features, of course).

If you installed Lion on a blank drive or partition, it'll need some more information to get you up and running. You'll have to select your country keyboard layout and time zone (Lion can do this for you; you'll see a checkbox labeled "Set time zone automatically using current location").

Then you'll be offered the opportunity to transfer data from another Mac. If you chose not to, click Continue. Next, Lion will try to connect to the Internet. It'll automatically choose a network option, but if you're not happy with Lion's choice, click the Different Network Setup button in the lower left of the window and choose your preferred network.

Once you're hooked up to the network, you'll be asked for your Apple ID. You can skip this step, but if you have a MobileMe or iCloud account, using that as your Apple ID will let your Mac use the associated services without you having to do any more configuring. After you enter (or create) your Apple ID, you'll be offered the opportunity to register. The information you type into the registration form will be used not just to garner you a spot in Apple's database, but also to generate an address card for you in Address Book and to set up your email address for use with Mail.

Lion will then ask you for some info on how and where you intend to use your Mac. Once the data collection is out of the way, you'll be prompted to set up a user account. Lion will generate a full name and account name for you. If you don't want to use its suggestions, you can type in your own names. You'll also have to enter a password and, if you wish, a hint in case you forget the password.

With your account created, Lion will give you the chance to snap a picture for the account with a webcam or choose one from your picture library. Once that's done, Lion will configure your Mac using your MobileMe or iCloud information (if you use those services). If you're not a MobileMe or iCloud subscriber, don't worry—your Mac is ready to go. You just won't have the things that MobileMe and iCloud configure (like Mail, for example) automatically set up for you.

NOTE

If you're tight on disk space, there's no compelling reason to keep the installer around after you're done installing Lion. If you need the installer later, you can always download it again for free. And if the worst happens and you have to use Recovery Mode and reinstall Lion, having the installer on your Mac won't be of any help, since reinstalling with Recovery Mode means downloading Lion again.

Moving Data and Applications from Another Computer

Not everyone will install Lion from the Mac App Store; some folks will have a new Mac with Lion preinstalled. If you're one of these lucky ones, you aren't interested in how to install Lion. But if you're upgrading from an older Mac or from a Windows-based PC (getting data from a Windows PC onto your Mac is a new, very nifty feature of Lion), you'll certainly be interested in getting that mountain of data from your old machine onto your new computer. Apple has an app for that: Migration Assistant can transfer files, settings, and preferences from your old computer to your new one. After running Migration Assistant, your new Mac will seem a lot like your old Mac. If you're transferring data from a PC, your new Mac won't seem like your old PC, but it *will* have the PC's data on it.

NOTE

You might not want to migrate your data from an old computer right away: playing with a factory-fresh system is fun, and migrating data isn't a once-in-a-lifetime opportunity. Toy with your new Mac now, and then migrate your data later using Migration Assistant.

When you run Migration Assistant, it can transfer the following things to your new machine:

Users

All your user accounts will be moved to your new Mac. Accounts retain the same privileges (or restrictions) that they had before. If you try to move over a user that already exists on your Mac, you'll have the option to change the account's name or replace the existing user (as long as you aren't logged in as that user; if you want to import settings into your account, first use System Preferences→Accounts to create a new user, log in as that user, and then run Migration Assistant again). See the section "User Accounts" on page 35 for more information.

Applications

All the applications in the Applications folder are transferred. You won't have to reinstall your applications, and most should retain all their settings (including any registration or activation needed to run them).

Settings

Have a bunch of saved networks and passwords in your Network Preferences? They all come along for the ride. So, if you're used to automatically jumping on at the local WiFi hotspot, you'll get on without any extra effort. If your screensaver requires a password to get back to the desktop, it still will. There are three suboptions under Settings: Time Zone, Machine (computer settings other than network or time zone), and Network. Pick and choose the ones you want to move to your new machine.

Other files and folders

If your Mac has files strewn everywhere, even if they aren't where Mac OS X expects them to be (the Documents directory), they'll be transferred.

Migration Assistant doesn't move the following items:

The System folder
You're installing a new system, so you don't need the old System folder to come along.

Apple applications and utilities
Migration Assistant assumes that every Apple application (like FaceTime and iCal) on your Lion machine is newer or the same as the corresponding item on the Mac you're transferring data from, so those applications won't get moved. Instead, your Migration Assistant will keep the preferences the same and let you use the newer version. This is only a problem when you hate the latest version of iMovie (to cite one example). If you want to use the older version, you'll have to manually move it over.

As you'd probably guess, you need to be logged in as an administrative user (or be able to supply the username and password of an administrative user) to run Migration Assistant. Then go to Applications→Utilities→Migration Assistant to get started.

If you haven't migrated data since the MacBook Air came out, the process has changed a little bit. In the days before the Air, Migration Assistant used FireWire Target Disk Mode: you'd start the computer you wanted to transfer data from in this mode (by holding down ⌘-T while booting or choosing "Start in Target Disk Mode" from the Startup Disk preference pane), plug it into the destination Mac, and then Migration Assistant would take care of the rest. The good news is that this method still works if you have two computers with FireWire; the better news is that if you don't have two Macs with FireWire, you can still use Migration Assistant. In fact, Migration Assistant offers two ways to get your old data on your new Mac (shown in Figure 2-3):

From another Mac, PC, Time Machine backup, or other disk
> Choosing this option allows you to transfer data from a Mac or PC that's either wired to or on the same network (wired or wireless) as your new Lion-powered Mac.

To another Mac
> This option is the counterpart of the "From another Mac or PC" option—you select this one on your source machine, and the other on your destination machine.

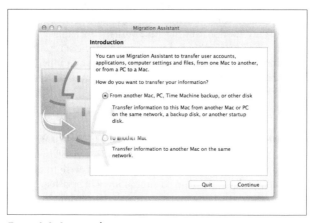

Figure 2-3. Starting the migration process

If you chose the first option, you'll get two *more* options to choose between:

From another Mac or PC

This is the option you'll use if you want to transfer data, well, from another Mac or PC. When you select this option and click the Continue button, the next screen will warn you that all your applications must be closed. Save anything you've been working on and click Continue, and your Mac will start looking for other computers to transfer data from. Unless you've used the "To another Mac" option (discussed above) on the computer you want to transfer data from, it won't find any. No problem: Migration Assistant will keep looking while you fire up Migration Assistant on the other machine and select "To another Mac" on that computer. Once both computers are on the same page, you'll see something like Figure 2-4.

Click Continue and you'll see a passcode. You don't have to write it down or remember it, you just need to make sure it's the same as the one displayed on the machine you are transferring data from. (The passcode won't show up on the data-donating machine until the exchange has been initiated by the Mac you are moving the data *to*.) Verify that the numbers match and then click continue. Next, you get a chance to decide what you want to transfer (see "Fine-Tuning Data Migration" on page 33). Click Continue and your data will be transferred.

From a Time Machine backup or other disk

If you choose this option, your new Mac will scan all attached drives and then present you with a list of drives you can migrate data from. Click the one you wish to use and then click Continue. By default, Lion will transfer all your relevant info, but you can change that behavior (see "Fine-Tuning Data Migration" on page 33).

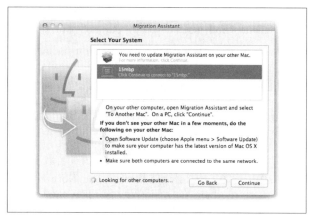

Figure 2-4. Getting data from an older Mac

NOTE

If both Macs have FireWire, choose "From a Time Machine backup or other disk" and then restart the Mac you want to get data *from* in FireWire Target Disk Mode by holding down the T key while the computer boots, until you see a FireWire symbol dancing on the screen.

Networking Options When Migrating Data

Before Migration Assistant came along, getting your data onto your new Mac could be a real pain. While Migration Assistant is a fantastic tool, it has one drawback: It doesn't differentiate between different types of networks.

As you already know, not every network connection is equal. If you're transferring small bits of information (like email or text messages), a cellphone protocol is plenty of bandwidth. But when you're transferring larger chunks of data, the type of connection is more important. If you're using Migration Assistant, there's a good chance that you're planning to send a bunch of data from your old computer to your new Mac, so the speed of the transfer really matters—especially since you'll be locked out of both machines for the duration of the transfer.

Here are your data-transfer options from fastest to slowest:

Ethernet
> Ethernet is your fastest option. If your Mac has an Ethernet port (all Macs except the MacBook Air do), you can string an Ethernet cable between your old computer and your new Mac and transfer data at up to a gigabit (1,000 Mb) per second.

FireWire 800
> FireWire 800 is your second-fastest option. Not every Mac that can run Lion has a FireWire 800 port, so if you're unsure, check out your System Information (see "System Information" on page 186) and select FireWire. If both your computers are FireWire 800 equipped, you'll be swapping data at a peppy 800 Mbps.

NOTE

A lot of Mac owners will have FireWire *400* on their old machine and FireWire *800* on their new one (no new Macs have FireWire 400). In that case, you can get a FireWire 400 to 800 cable (try Amazon) and then transfer your files using a 400 Mbps connection.

WiFi
> WiFi is the slowest option. Its speed varies depending on the network, but if you're using the 802.11n, your network could be running up to 300 Mbps.

You might be wondering why Thunderbolt, Apple's newest 10 Gbps dual-channel networking option) isn't listed. As of this writing, Thunderbolt isn't supported by Migration Assistant, though this could change as Thunderbolt becomes more common.

The speeds listed above are best-case scenarios, so your real-life experience may not match those numbers. But even with that caveat noted, you'll save a significant amount of time if you use one of the wired options instead of WiFi.

Your Mac is kind of lazy. It doesn't care which transfer method is the fastest; it'll automatically opt for the network connection you're currently using. So if you don't want to sling files over your WiFi connection (which could take forever), you can string an Ethernet cable between your Macs and then switch to *that* connection in the Network preference pane to get your data moving at breakneck speed.

Fine-Tuning Data Migration

If you're migrating data, chances are you have a new Mac. If you're like most people, you've accumulated a lot of cruft over time, and you might not want to transfer *everything* from your old Mac. Of course you'll want to save that folder of LOLcat pictures, but that folder with your master's thesis is just taking up space.

Migration Assistant lets you decide what to take and what to leave behind in terms of users and settings. (Don't worry: this is a nondestructive process, so the data you shun on your new Mac will still be on the old Mac.) Simply follow the data-migration process described earlier in this chapter, but when you get to the "Select Items to Migrate" screen (Figure 2-5), uncheck the items you want to leave behind. Click the disclosure triangle to display all your options.

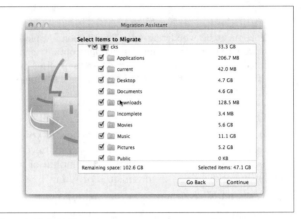

Figure 2-5. Deciding what you want on your new Mac

After you make your selections, click Continue and your data will be transferred. Give it some time and your data will magically appear on your new Mac.

NOTE

Don't get confused by the folder names. For example, Movies doesn't mean that Migration Assistant will import all your movie files, just that it will import the Movies *folder*. If you have movies stored elsewhere and you want them to come along during the transfer, make sure the "All other files and folders" option is checked.

Once Migration Assistant finishes migrating your data, Setup Assistant will pop up and offer to upgrade your email (if you're migrating from an older version of Mac OS X). This takes a few moments, but once it's finished, you're free to use your new Mac and pick up where you left off with the old one!

CHAPTER 3

A Quick Guide to Lion

What You Need to Know About Mac OS X

Finding your way around Lion for the first time is exciting, but it's also easy to miss out on many cool new features, especially if you're new to Mac OS X or you've been using an older version of the operating system. This chapter will get you up to speed on the basics of Mac OS X, with a special focus on what's new in Lion. It'll familiarize you with the most important aspects of Mac OS X so you can get the most out of Apple's best operating system to date. The logical place to start is with the first thing you created when you installed or ran Mac OS X for the first time—your account.

User Accounts

Lion is the latest and greatest from Apple, but the operating system's roots go all the way to Unix, a multiuser workstation and server operating system. Because Mac OS X is based on Unix, it's also multiuser to its core. Even if no one but you ever touches your Mac, it's still helpful to understand user accounts, because you may need to deal with them someday. Consider these situations:

- As you'll learn shortly, you may want to set up an unprivileged account for day-to-day use to limit your vulnerability to mistakes and malicious software.

- If you ever need to run a demonstration on your Mac, you'll probably want to create a separate account to run the demo to prevent interruptions from chat buddies, calendar reminders, and the like.

- Even the most solitary Mac user eventually needs to let someone else use her Mac (a houseguest, family member, or TSA agent), and it's so easy to set up a new user account that you may as well do it—then even your most reckless friend can use your Mac without much threat of major chaos.

There are five types of user accounts in Mac OS X, and you can also create groups of users:

Administrator

When you create your first account in Mac OS X, it'll automatically be an Administrator account. This is the most powerful account because an administrator can make *global* changes that affect the computer and all other user accounts, like adding and removing programs. Because of this ability to change things (sometimes inadvertently), most savvy Mac users argue that you shouldn't use Administrator accounts for day-to-day computing; instead, they recommend using a Standard account most of the time.

NOTE

You might detest the idea of jettisoning the power of the Administrator account for day-to-day use. But even if you're using a Standard account, you can still make global changes by typing in your Administrator account name and password.

Standard

Standard accounts are the sweet spot: you can't mess up your Mac or anyone else's account while using a Standard account, but you still have plenty of control over how your Mac works. You can add and delete programs for just your account, but not to the entire system, and you can delete files you own (those you've created or installed), but not files owned by others.

Managed with Parental Controls

Accounts managed with Parental Controls are limited in what they can do. These users can't make changes to the system at all. If you tried to use a managed account, you'd likely find it frustrating and unacceptable. But to a five-year-old, a managed account is nirvana. You can adjust the settings with the Parental Controls preference pane (see "Parental Controls" on page 149).

Sharing Only

Sharing Only accounts are designed to let people connect to your machine from another computer to share files. People assigned this type of account can't log into your Mac via the login screen; only remote connections are accepted.

Guest

In Snow Leopard you had to specifically enable this type of account, but in Lion it's automatically available. This type of account is fantastic if you want to let someone use your Mac without being able to make any permanent changes. Log someone in as a Guest and he'll be able to search the Web, check his email online, and much more. But the moment he logs out, everything he did—any data he downloaded, for example—is gone. You can even enable Parental Controls for a Guest account if you're worried about guests doing things you'd rather they didn't.

Group

You can use Group accounts to create a collection of multiple users. You can use these types of accounts to exercise fine-grained control over privileges for shared documents.

Lion will also allow one more type of access for your Mac: once iCloud comes out (it wasn't out when this book went to press), you'll have the option to enable the Find My Mac service. If you do, not only will you be able to locate your lost Mac over the Web, but anyone who finds it will only be able to start the computer in Safari-only mode. So all that person will be able to do is browse the Web with Safari, and while they're using your Mac, location information will be sent to the Web to help you find your computer.

Setting up accounts

Now that you know the different types of accounts in Lion, you'll likely want to set up a few accounts. Click **⌘**→System Preferences→Users & Groups (located in the System section). Before you can make any changes, you have to click the lock icon at the bottom left of the preference pane, and then enter an administrator username and password. The extra level of security is there because this preference pane lets you adjust the level of access for other accounts, so you wouldn't want an unauthorized person making changes here.

To add a new account, click the + button above the lock icon. This opens a drop-down window where you can select the type of account to create, type in the identifying info (full name, account name), and set up a password. If you want to choose a picture for the new user, after you create the account, select it in the list on the preference pane's left and then, in the middle of the pane, click the account's picture and choose Edit Picture. You'll get the option of using a saved picture (click Choose) or taking one with your Mac's built-in iSight camera or an attached webcam.

To disable the Guest account, click it in the list of accounts, and then uncheck the box marked "Allow guests to log in to this computer." This will prevent guests from using your computer without a password.

The Home Folder

The Home folder is what makes your Mac seem like *your* Mac. For example, if you create a document and save it in Documents, the document doesn't show up in some centralized documents folder for the entire system, it shows up in the folder called Documents that lives inside your Home folder.

This pattern extends to other folders, too (Music, Movies, Pictures, and more). Each account you create gets its own Home folder with a subset of folders inside it. This is where all your files and personal preferences (like your selected desktop background) are stored.

NOTE

There's one folder in Users that doesn't correspond to any user: the Shared folder. You can use it to store files and folders you need to share between users on the same Mac.

You can access your Home folder by opening a Finder window and then either clicking the house icon in the sidebar or choosing Go→Home (Shift-⌘-H). In every Home folder, you'll find the following subfolders:

Desktop
> This is where all the files sitting on your desktop are stored. (There are a few other types of items that can appear on the desktop—hard disks, CDs, DVDs, iPods, and servers—but you won't see them in this folder.) If you drag a document from this folder to the Trash, it'll disappear from your desktop.

Documents
> This is the default location where your Mac saves documents. Using this folder isn't mandatory, but it does offer a level of convenience to have a central repository for all your documents. You can add subfolders for even more

organization: just open the Documents folder and then choose File→New Folder (Shift-⌘-N).

Downloads

The Downloads folder serves double duty: it's a folder in your Home directory and it has a spot in your Dock. Anything you download from the Web via a browser shows up here (unless you change the default download location in your browser's preferences, that is) *and* in your Dock in the Downloads stack (the stack bounces when a new item finishes downloading). If you click the Save button next to an attachment in Mail, it's also saved here. You can get your downloaded items either by opening this folder or by going to the Downloads stack in the Dock.

Movies

This folder is much like the Documents folder, only it stores all the movies you make with iMovie and screencasts you make with QuickTime Player. Just as with the Documents folder, there's no reason to store your movies here other than convenience.

Music

The Music folder, not surprisingly, is where you can store music files. It's also where iTunes stores its music library and any iTunes purchases you make, including iPhone/iPod apps and videos.

Pictures

Toss all your *.jpg*, *.png*, and *.gif* files right in here. iPhoto also uses this folder to store images you add to iPhoto.

Public

The Public folder is a repository for files you want to share with other users who can log into your Mac. You can get to another user's Public folder by opening a Finder window and choosing Go→Computer. You'll see a window showing all the drives and networks coupled to the Mac you're using. Selecting the startup drive will reveal a folder called Users. Open that folder and you'll see all the other users' Home folders (they're labeled with the respective user's names, as shown in Figure 3-1). Open the appropriate person's folder and you'll see her Public folder. You can grab any files stored in another user's Public folder and use them as you wish. Likewise, any files you toss into your Public folder can be grabbed by anyone using the same Mac. (Note that, while you can share any files you find in the Public folder, you can't actually change the contents of someone else's Public folder.) If you want to share files in this folder with people on *other* computers, you'll have to go to the Sharing preference pane (see "Sharing" on page 145).

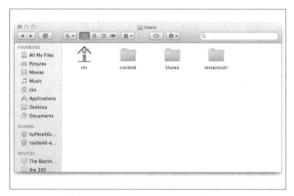

Figure 3-1. All your Mac's accounts in one place

To receive files from others, have them put the files in your Drop Box, a folder inside the Public folder. Drop Box is a shared folder, but the sharing only goes one way: people can put things into your Drop Box, but they can't take anything out. In fact, they can't even see what's in this folder. To use Drop Box, enable File Sharing (see "Sharing" on page 145).

Sites

You'll only see this folder if you're using an Administrator account. If you want your Mac to host a website (it's certainly capable), this is where you put the files for the site. You'll need to do more than add an HTML file to this folder to get your site working, though. See "Sharing" on page 145 to start sharing sites stored in this folder over your local network.

Where's My Library Folder?

In previous editions of OS X, there was one additional folder in your Home folder: Library. This is where your preferences and settings (among other things) are stored. If you're used to manually controlling aspects of your Library folder, you'll likely miss having easy access to it.

It turns out the Library folder isn't really gone; it's just invisible. The easiest way to make it appear is to head to the Finder and click the Go menu; with the menu open, press the Option key, and the Library folder will magically appear as a menu item. Now you can get back to manually messing about with your Library folder if you're so inclined (but be warned that tweaking items in the Library folder can have unintended consequences).

Using Lion

Once you have Lion running and your system set up, what do you need to know to use it? This section teaches you the basics of starting up your Mac, getting around after you've booted, and shutting the machine down.

Starting Up

Chapter 2 covered what happens when you turn on a fresh, out-of-the-box Mac (or a new install of Lion). Each time you boot up your Mac after that, the startup experience is usually seamless. As you'd expect, your Mac will boot into Lion (unless you tell it otherwise).

NOTE

If you've installed Boot Camp (see "Boot Camp Assistant" on page 179) or another operating system, you can set the default startup disk with the Startup Disk preference pane (see "Startup Disk" on page 155).

The first thing you'll see when you start your Mac is the gray Apple logo (), followed by the spinning wheel that resembles a circle of perpetually falling dominoes. Once your Mac finishes booting, you'll be logged in. (If you've disabled automatic login, you'll instead be presented with a list of users or a username/password prompt, depending on your settings; see "Logging In" on page 44 for more details. Log in and you'll be transported to Mac OS X.)

Thanks to Resume, all the apps that were running when you last turned off your Mac will automatically open with all the windows you had before. But you don't have to use Resume if you don't want to. When you shut down or log out of your Mac, the dialog box that appears includes a "Reopen windows when logging back in" checkbox (Figure 3-2). Uncheck the box and you'll end up at your desktop, with no windows in sight.

Figure 3-2. Uncheck this box to keep those pesky windows from reopening

Startup key commands

Before you start booting up your Mac, you can press and hold one of these keys/key combinations to change how it starts (useful when troubleshooting).

Key command	Action
Hold mouse button while powering on	Ejects any media in the optical drive
C	Forces your Mac to start up from a CD or DVD in the optical drive
R	Resets display for Macs with built-in displays (MacBooks and iMacs) back to the factory settings
T	If the Mac has a FireWire port, boots the Mac in FireWire Target Disk Mode; to get out of this mode, restart the Mac
⌘-S	Boots in Single User Mode, which starts your Mac with a text-only console where you can perform some expert-level system maintenance
⌘-V	Boots in verbose mode, which shows all the kernel and startup messages while your Mac is booting
Shift	Boots in Safe Mode, a reduced functionality mode that forces your Mac to check your startup disk, load only the most important kernel extensions, disable fonts not in the */System/Library/Fonts* folder, and more
Option	Invokes Startup Manager and allows you to select which OS to boot into; useful if you have multiple copies of Mac OS X installed or use Boot Camp to run other operating systems

Logging In

By default, your Mac is set up to automatically log in as the user you created when you first set up your machine. This is something of a security risk, since it means that anyone can get into your Administrator account simply by powering up your Mac. If multiple people use your machine, you'll likely want to turn this option off. To do that, click →System Preferences→Users & Groups. Click the lock icon in the preference pane's bottom left, enter your password, and then click Login Options and change the "Automatic login" setting to Off.

The Login Options are also where you can control fast user switching. This feature lets you switch users without having to log off, so the applications that you have running keep going while another user logs into her account. However, having more than one user logged in can use up quite a bit of memory, so if you have less than 2 GB of RAM, you might want to turn this feature off.

If you leave fast user switching on, look for an icon or username on the right side of the menu bar. Click this name or icon and use the drop-down menu to select another user to log in as. If you turn fast user switching off, you'll have to log out (⌘→Log Out) before you can log in as a different user.

Logging Out, Sleeping, and Shutting Down

Using the Mac is great, but at some point you'll want to *stop* using it. When you reach that point, you've got options:

Shut Down

> To shut down your Mac, click ⌘→Shut Down. Click Shut Down in the dialog box that appears (or do nothing for one minute), and your Mac will power off. It should only take a few seconds to do so. The next time you want to use your Mac, hit the power button and wait for the machine to boot.

Log Out

> To close your current work session and quit all running programs but leave your Mac running, log out by clicking ⌘→Log Out or by pressing Shift-⌘-Q. Then click Log Out in the dialog box that appears. Pressing Shift-Option-⌘-Q instead logs you out immediately—there's no confirmation dialog box. To use your Mac again, you (or another user) will need to log in.

Sleep

You don't have to shut your Mac down every day; you can just let it sleep. To put a MacBook to sleep, all you have to do is close the lid. On desktop Macs, select →Sleep or press Option-⌘-⏏ (these methods work on MacBooks, too). A sleeping Mac uses very little electricity, and it'll wake up in seconds. (For more on saving energy, see "Energy Saver" on page 132.) Wondering if your Mac is sleeping or simply off? On MacBooks, you'll see an indicator light that pulses to let you know it's only sleeping.

Shut down and log out shortcuts

No one wants to spend lots of time logging out or shutting down. Here are some shortcuts that make the process faster.

Key command	Action
Shift-⌘-Q	Logs you out
Shift-Option-⌘-Q	Logs you out without a confirmation dialog box
→Shut Down	Shuts your Mac down; hold Option when selecting this menu item (or press Control-Option-⌘-⏏ instead) to shut down immediately
→Restart	Restarts your Mac; hold Option when selecting this menu item (or press Control-⌘-⏏ instead) to restart immediately
Control-⏏	Displays a window that lets you restart, put to sleep, or shut down your Mac
Control-⌘-Power Button	Forces your Mac to shut down (use this only as a last resort)
Option-⌘-⏏	Puts your Mac to sleep

Lion Basics

A lot happens between when you start up your Mac and when you shut it down. The time you spend in Mac OS X will be more pleasant and productive if you learn where everything is. The logical place to start the tour is right at the top of your screen, with the menu bar.

The Menu Bar

The menu bar spans the top of your monitor (if you use multiple monitors, you can choose which one the menu bar shows up on with the Displays preference pane). The left side of the bar provides access to commonly used commands and the right side is reserved for menu extras (see "Menu extras" on page 55) and Spotlight (the magnifying glass icon). Every Mac user's menu bar is likely to look a little different, depending on what's installed and how the Mac is configured. A typical menu bar is shown in Figure 3-3.

Figure 3-3. A typical menu bar

Here's what you'll find in the menu bar, from left to right:

1. The Apple menu ()
2. The Application menu
3. A set of application-related menus
4. Menu extras
5. Spotlight

The Apple menu

No matter which application you're using, the options in the
 menu are always the same (see Figure 3-4).

Figure 3-4. Lion's Apple menu

Here's what each menu item does:

About This Mac

Pops up a window giving you a quick overview of your
Mac: the version of Mac OS X it's running, the processor
it has, and the amount of RAM that's installed. There are
three things you can click in this window:

- Click the version number (such as 10.7) to cycle through the build number of Mac OS X and the serial number of your Mac. (It's not unusual to need this info when getting support over the phone.)

- Click Software Update to see whether you have all the latest and greatest updates installed.

- Click More Info to open System Information. This option has been improved in Lion. When you select it, you'll see tabs that give you an overview of your Mac, and ones that tell you (in a cool graphic fashion) about Displays, Storage (drives attached to your Mac), and Memory (how much you have installed and in which slot). You'll also find tabs for Support (this is a good starting point when you're problem solving) and Service, which lets you check your warranty status and gives you a chance to buy AppleCare (Apple's extended warranty service).

Software Update
> Launches Software Update and checks for changes to Apple-supplied software (it doesn't check for updates to third-party software).

App Store
> Launches the Mac App Store, where you can look for new applications, check for updates to ones you already have, and so on.

System Preferences
> Launches System Preferences, which is covered in detail in Chapter 5.

Dock
> Opens a menu that lets you quickly configure your Dock: Turn Hiding On, Turn Magnification On, and three Dock positioning options (you can put it anywhere but the top of your screen). The Dock Preferences option, not surprisingly, opens the Dock preference pane. For more info, see "Dock" on page 121.

Recent Items

Displays a menu showing your 10 most recently used applications, 10 most recently opened documents, and 10 most recently used servers. You can change the number of items that are displayed here by going to System Preferences→General, and then adjusting the "Number of recent items" settings.

Force Quit

Forces stubborn applications to quit. For more on this command, see the section "Misbehaving Applications" on page 100.

Sleep

Puts your Mac into sleep mode, a low-power mode that preserves what you were doing before you put your machine to sleep. When you wake your Mac up, everything will be just as you left it. To wake a sleeping Mac, just press a key or move the mouse.

You can set your Mac to automatically sleep after a period of inactivity by using the Energy Saver preference pane (see "Energy Saver" on page 132).

Restart

Makes your Mac shut down and then immediately reboot and go through the entire startup process. You'll be asked to confirm that you really want to restart your Mac. If you don't click Cancel, your Mac will restart one minute after you select this menu option.

Shut Down

Powers your Mac down. It'll stay shut down until you press the power button, unless you've set a time for your Mac to auto-start in the Energy Saver preference pane (see "Energy Saver" on page 132).

Log Out

Logs you out of your user account. The next time someone uses your Mac, he or she will have to log in.

The Application menu

Next to the menu is the Application menu. The name and contents of this menu depend on what application you're currently using. Figure 3-5 shows the Finder's Application menu.

Figure 3-5. The Finder's Application menu

There really isn't a standard Application menu, but most have some commonalities. In a typical Application menu you'll find:

About [Application Name]
Opens a window with the application's version number, copyright info, and whatever else the program's developer thinks should be there.

Preferences

Opens the application's preferences window. What you can control from this window varies from application to application—it could be very little or a lot. For info on the Finder's preferences, see the section "Mastering the Finder" on page 59.

Services

All the services the current app can use appear in a list when you highlight this option. Check out "The Services Menu" on page 53 for details.

Hide [Application Name]

Hides all of the current application's windows. If you have 50 Safari windows open and don't want to manually minimize each one to see what lies beneath, choose this option. To get the windows back, just click the application's Dock icon.

Hide Others

Hides every application except the one you're using.

Show All

This is the antidote to the Hide command. If you've hidden a single application or every application, Show All will return all the hidden application windows to full visibility.

Quit [Application Name]

Quits the current application. (You can also invoke this command by pressing ⌘-Q.) Most people's inclination is to quit any application they aren't using, but that often isn't necessary. Mac OS X is very good at allocating resources, so leaving an application idling will generally have very little impact on the system.

The Services Menu

The Services menu is the most complex option in the Application menu. It offers you quick access to functions provided by other programs, which are called services. The services available to you depend on the applications installed on your Mac and the program you're using. TextEdit (which you can find in the Applications folder) provides a nice example of what the Services menu can do. Figure 3-6 shows the options available when you've selected some text in TextEdit. If you want to send the selected text as a Mail message, for example, all you need to do is choose New Email With Selection, and Mail will pop open a new message with the text already inserted.

In some applications, the Services menu won't have anything to offer (the menu will read "No Services Apply").

Clicking the Services Preferences option opens the Keyboard preference pane to its Services section, where you can customize the Services menu. You can also create your own services with Automator (see "Automator" on page 160).

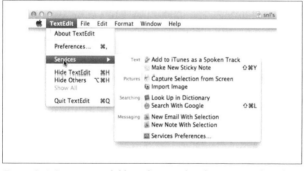

Figure 3-6. Services available with TextEdit when text is selected

Standard Application menus

After the Application menu come more menus. How many? That depends on the application. For example, Mail has eight and Safari has seven. You'll find at least four menus in the menu bar besides the Application menu. What's in these four menus *also* depends on the application, but there are some standard options to expect:

File

This menu typically contains options for saving, opening, creating, and printing files.

Edit

Here you'll find the old Mac standbys: Cut (⌘-X), Copy (⌘-C), Paste (⌘-V), and Undo (⌘-Z).

Window

This menu lists all the open windows for the current application.

Help

Depending on the application and its developer, this menu can either be very useful or a waste of space. When you open the Help menu (either by clicking it or by pressing Shift-⌘-?), you'll see a search box and a few other options. One of the really nice things about the Help menu in Mac OS X is that it won't just regurgitate an entry in a database—instead, if possible, it *shows* you how to do what you want to do. For example, suppose you want to create a new folder while using the Finder. Open the Finder's Help menu, type **new folder** in the search box, and then hover your cursor over the New Folder entry in the list that appears. The Help system will then show you which menu contains the New Folder option and highlight it with a floating blue arrow, as shown in Figure 3-7.

Figure 3-7. Help can find the menu item you need.

Menu extras

The right side of the menu bar is where you'll find the menu extras, a.k.a. menulets. (Spotlight is on the bar's *far* right and isn't technically a menu extra.) Menu extras give you easy access to functions you use often. The menu extra's icon usually reflects what it does. A useful example is the Keychain menu extra (Figure 3-8), which you can add by launching the Keychain Access utility in */Applications/Utilities* and then choosing "Show keychain status in menu bar" from its preferences. It gives you quick access to your passwords and secure notes without having to make a trip to the Utilities folder.

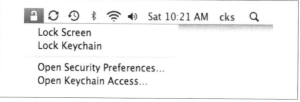

Figure 3-8. The Keychain menu extra

Not every menu extra is a shortcut to a program; some control settings (such as the Volume menu extra) and some are there to show the status of certain aspects of your Mac (such as the Battery menu extra). What menu extras you find useful depends on how you use your Mac.

Unlike menus, whose options change depending on the application you're using, menu extras remain constant: each one always does the same thing, no matter which program is running.

The menu extras you see by default depend on how your Mac is configured. You can banish unwanted menu extras by ⌘-dragging them off the menu bar; the menu extra will disappear with a satisfying poof sound and an accompanying animation. To reorder your menu extras, ⌘-drag them into any order you want. Note that you can't move the Spotlight icon—it looks like a menu extra, but as far as Mac OS X is concerned, it's immovable and permanent.

The Accounts menu

If you've enabled fast user switching (see "Users & Groups" on page 148), you'll see the name or icon of the current user here. Click it to select another user to log in as.

Spotlight

Clicking this magnifying glass icon brings up the Spotlight search box. For more information, see "Searching with Spotlight" on page 91.

Use the menu bar less

If you really want to be productive, it's much quicker to use keyboard shortcuts for most commands than to go hunting for them in the menu bar. Here's a list of some of the most commonly used keyboard shortcuts for items in the menu bar.

Key command	Action
⌘-C	Copies selected information to the clipboard
⌘-V	Pastes the contents of the clipboard into the current document
⌘-X	Cuts the current selection and copies it to the clipboard
⌘-A	Selects everything (the entire document, all items in a folder, etc.)
⌘-S	Saves the current file (you can't use this one too often)
⌘-O	Opens a new file
⌘-W	Closes the current window
⌘-Z	Undoes your most recent action (some programs offer multiple levels of undo)
⌘-H	Hides the current application and its windows
⌘-,	Opens the current application's Preferences window
⌘-Q	Quits the current program (not available in Finder)

There are many more key commands at your disposal (see Chapter 8), but these are likely to be the ones you use most often. (As well, each application has its own keyboard shortcuts that can streamline your workflow, so learning the key commands for the programs you use frequently is worth your time.)

The Desktop

As you probably know, the big area under the menu bar is called the desktop. Open application windows float over the desktop. Depending on how you have it configured, the desktop will also show you all the attached and internal drives (iPods, flash drives, and so on), any optical disks (CDs, DVDs), and any files you've stored here for easy access. You can change your desktop's background either by Control-clicking or right-clicking the desktop and then choosing Change Desktop Background, or by heading to the Desktop & Screen Saver preference pane (see "Desktop & Screen Saver" on page 118).

To control how items are displayed on the desktop, choose Show View Options from the Finder's View menu, or press ⌘-J. The window shown in Figure 3-9 appears.

Figure 3-9. The desktop's view options

The Desktop view options window lets you control the size of desktop icons (from 16×16 pixels all the way to 128×128 pixels), how they're spaced (there's an invisible grid that Mac OS X uses when arranging desktop icons), and the size and location of their labels.

If you check the "Show item info" box, you'll see extra information when looking at items on your desktop. Drives show the name of the drive and the amount of free space left, folders list the name of the folder and the number of items contained, and DVDs show the amount of data stored on them. The extra information displayed for files depends on their type. Images, for example, display the size of the image.

The "Show icon preview" box lets you toggle between generic icons and icons that display the file's contents. The "Sort by" menu lets you choose how desktop icons are arranged. You can have them snap to the (invisible) grid or be arranged according to some criteria (name, date created, and so on).

To navigate on the desktop without using the mouse, you can use the arrow keys. Another option is to start typing an item's name; the item will automatically get highlighted and you can open it by pressing ⌘-O. Hitting the Return key instead allows you to rename the item.

To control what kind of items appear on the desktop, you use the Finder's preferences (switch to the Finder and then choose Finder→Preferences or hit ⌘-,). Under the General tab, you'll find options to display (or hide) hard disks; external disks; CDs, DVDs, and iPods; and connected servers.

Mastering the Finder

Understanding the Finder is key to successfully getting around in Mac OS X. It lets you move files, copy files, and launch applications, among other things. The most common way users interact with the Finder is through a Finder window.

The Finder window

The Finder window has undergone some substantial changes in Lion: gone are the search options in the sidebar and the bar at the bottom that used to include a summary of the current folder and a slider to adjust icon size. Also missing are the colorful sidebar icons; now, as in Mail, everything is muted. Finally, though you probably won't miss it, the "Hide/Show toolbar and sidebar" button is gone.

To bring the Finder to the front, click some empty space on the desktop, click the Finder's Dock icon, or hit ⌘-Tab until you select its icon. Once the Finder is frontmost, hit ⌘-N to open a Finder window. Figure 3-10 shows a typical one.

NOTE

If you upgraded to Lion from Snow Leopard, your Finder window will look slightly different. Exactly what you'll see depends on how you configured the window in Snow Leopard, but some of the buttons may be in different spots. You'll also see the Quick Look button, which has an eye icon and lets you peek at the selected file (see "Common Finder tasks" on page 68 for details).

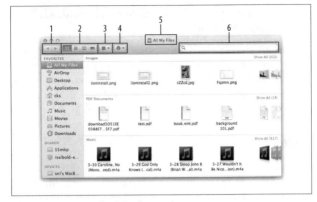

Figure 3-10. A standard Finder window

The Finder window is made up of several components:

1. Back and Forward buttons

These buttons cycle you through directories you've been using. For example, say you start in your Home directory and then drill down into your Documents folder. After you find the document you were looking for, clicking the back button returns you to your Home directory.

2. View controls

These buttons control how the Finder displays information. You have four options: Icon View (the default), List View, Column View, and Cover Flow; see "Finder views" on page 65.

3. Action menu

Clicking this button reveals a drop-down menu that varies depending on the item selected. Generally, it contains the same options you'd get if you right-clicked or Control-clicked that item.

4. Arrange menu

This button lets you change the order in which the items in a folder are displayed. Clicking it gives you nine different sorting options (plus the option to not sort at all).

5. *Proxy icon*

This item is a graphical representation of your current location (for example, the drawer icon in Figure 3-10 shows that you're in All My Files). Right-click or Control-click it to bring up a list of common destinations; select one to hop to that spot or drag a folder onto the list to create a copy of it in that location.

6. *Search box*

Enter text in this box and hit Return to tell the Finder to search for matching items. New in Lion, when you start typing a search term, it displays a drop-down menu with suggestions to help refine your search. The search is powered by Spotlight, but unlike a Spotlight search, it won't return Mail messages or web pages.

Customizing the Finder toolbar

To remove items from the Finder's toolbar, simply ⌘-drag them off of the toolbar. Doing this tidies things up, but it doesn't give you what most people want: *more* options. To add things to the toolbar, either right-click or Control-click on a blank space in the toolbar and select Customize Toolbar, or go to View→Customize Toolbar. The dialog box in Figure 3-11 opens, showing all the items you can add.

Figure 3-11. That's a lot of options!

Most of the items you can add are self-explanatory, but a few are worthy of a closer look:

Path

This button gives you a menu that shows the path up from the current directory to the top-level of your computer. For example, suppose you have the Finder open to your Pictures folder. Clicking this button will reveal the following list:

- Pictures
- [Your Home folder]
- Users
- [Your Boot Drive]
- [Your Computer]

You can choose any item in the list to jump to that directory.

Burn

Burn a lot of disks? This button can save you a lot of time. Select an item (or folder) and then click this button, and the Finder will tell you to insert a disk to burn to.

Get Info

This brings up the Info window for the selected item—very useful if you adjust permissions often.

The sidebar

The sidebar occupies the left-hand side of a Finder window and is reminiscent of iTunes's sidebar. The Finder divides the sidebar into three sections:

Favorites

This section lists the most common things you'll use: All My Files, AirDrop, Applications, Desktop, Documents, Downloads, Movies, Music, and Pictures. Some of these items point to actual folders (like Applications, for example), but not all of them do. All My Files points to all the files you've created; it's a Smart folder (see "Smart Folders" on page 85). AirDrop is a quick way to share files between Macs; see "AirDrop" on page 11 for details on using it.

Shared

This section lists any shared devices available to your Mac. Computers shared via Bonjour, shared drives, Time Capsule, Back to My Mac, and the like will show up here.

Devices

This is where you will find the devices connected to your Mac, including internal drives, your iDisk (if you have one), external drives, USB sticks, iPods, CDs, and DVDs.

The sidebar is more than just a speedy way to hop to these locations. Want to install an application you just downloaded? Instead of opening a Finder window to the Applications folder, just drag the application to the Applications folder in the sidebar. To reorder items in the sidebar, simply drag them around; to remove items, just drag them off of the sidebar. (Dragging an item out of the sidebar doesn't delete the item, it only deletes the reference to it from the sidebar.) You can do even more by right-clicking or Control-clicking an entry in the sidebar—a menu will pop allowing you to do some common and useful tasks tailored to the item you clicked. Finally, if you want quick access to a folder, application, or document, you can drag it to the sidebar and an alias will be created pointing to the item.

Finder preferences

Like every application, the Finder has a set of preferences you can customize. To access them, go to Finder→Preferences, or type ⌘-, while the Finder is the active application. The window that appears has four tabs:

General

Here's where you determine what items show up on your desktop. Your options are hard disks; external disks; CDs, DVDs, and iPods; and connected servers. You can also specify what directory a new Finder window opens to. The default is All My Files (see "All My Files" on page 10), but you can change that to any folder with the "New Finder windows show" menu. You also get a checkbox (that's unchecked by default) where you can choose to open folders in a new window. Finally, you can fine-tune (or turn off) spring-loaded folders, which automatically pop open if you drag an item over them, allowing you to quickly access nested folders while dragging an item.

Labels

If you're big on organization, you can label items with colors. By default, the labels' names match their colors—for example, if you label something with the color red, the text label is Red. That isn't very descriptive, so if you want to have the red label read "En Fuego" instead, this is where you can change the label name. (Note that changing a label's name won't impact how labeled folders are displayed.) To add a label to a folder, right-click or Control-click the folder and then choose the label you want to use from the menu that pops up.

Sidebar

This tab allows you to specify which items are displayed in the sidebar. If you've deleted a built-in item from the sidebar, a trip to this tab can restore it. If you uncheck all the items in a category, that category will no longer appear in the sidebar. (If you've added any items to a section of the sidebar, that category won't vanish until you also remove those items by dragging them out of the sidebar.)

Advanced

The Advanced tab gives you checkboxes to control whether filename extensions are displayed (if you check this box, Safari will be displayed as Safari.app, for example), whether the Finder should warn you before changing

---

an extension, whether you should be warned before emptying the Trash, and whether the Trash should be emptied securely. (See "Trash" on page 79 for more info.)

Finder views

You can change how items are displayed in the Finder by clicking the toolbar buttons (see "Customizing the Finder toolbar" on page 61) or using the keyboard shortcuts listed below. Here are your options:

Icon View (⌘-1)

This is the default view in Lion. Items are displayed as file icons, application icons, or folder icons (Figure 3-12). Single-clicking an item in Icon View selects it; double-clicking launches the application, opens the file (inside its associated application), or opens the folder. You can use the arrow keys to move from item to item. Holding the Shift key while using the arrow keys selects multiple items.

Figure 3-12. Icon view of the Applications folder

List View (⌘-2)

This view presents the contents of a folder as a list. You can open subfolders by clicking their disclosure triangles (see Figure 3-13). List View offers more information than Icon View, but feels more cluttered. As with Icon View, you can navigate through List View using the arrow keys:

↑ and ↓ change what's selected; → and ← open and close (respectively) a subfolder's disclosure triangle. To open all subfolders under the one that's selected, use Option-→; to close all subfolders after you've opened them, use Option-←. To sort files, click a row heading; the triangle in the heading indicates the order of the sort.

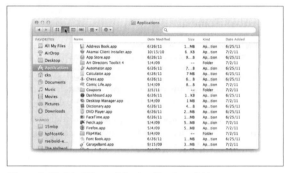

Figure 3-13. List View of the Applications folder

Column View (⌘-3)

Column View (Figure 3-14) is the favorite of a lot of users. While it looks a little like List View, it doesn't include any disclosure triangles. Clicking a folder in this view reveals the contents of that folder. If you continue all the way to a file, the last column will show a Quick Look preview of the file and some key information about the file. For example, if you drill down to a movie, the film's preview will appear in the last column, and you can even start playing it. If you select an application, the last column will display a huge version of the program's icon and information about the application.

In Column View, the arrow keys work exactly as you'd expect, moving the selection either up, down, left, or right. Holding Shift while pressing ↑ or ↓ allows you to select multiple items in the same directory.

You can change the width of the columns by dragging the two tiny vertical lines at the bottom of the dividers between columns. Hold Option as you drag to resize all the columns at once.

Figure 3-14. Column view of the Applications folder

Cover Flow View (⌘-4)

Cover Flow View first appeared in Leopard, and it's very slick. If you use iTunes, an iPod Touch, or an iPhone, you're familiar with this view, shown in Figure 3-15. It displays the items in a directory as large icons. You can adjust the size of the Cover Flow area by dragging the three tiny horizontal bars below the previews; Lion will resize the icons accordingly.

In this view, the ↑ and ← keys move the selection up in the list below the Cover Flow area, whereas the → and ↓ keys move your selection down that list.

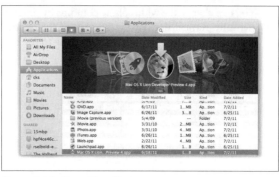

Figure 3-15. Cover Flow View

Common Finder tasks

You'll end up using the Finder for many basic tasks. Want to rename a folder? Copy or move files? The Finder is your best friend. Here are some common tasks you'll likely use the Finder for:

Rename a file, folder, or drive
> In the Finder, simply click the icon of whatever you want to rename and then press Return. Lion highlights the name so you can type a new one. Hit Return again to make the name stick.

Create a folder
> To create a new folder, you can either choose File→New Folder from the Finder's menu bar, or press Shift-⌘-N. The new folder appears as a subfolder of whatever folder you're currently using. New folders are creatively named "untitled folder."

Quickly look inside a file
> You can get a pop-up preview of a file's contents by using Quick Look. In the Finder, select a file, and then press Space or ⌘-Y (if there's a button with an eye icon in your Finder toolbar, you can also click that). An easy-on-the-eyes window (like the one in Figure 3-16) pops up, displaying the contents of the file.

Figure 3-16. Using Quick Look to watch Brian Jepson's favorite movie

Quick Look is file savvy; look at a Word document and you'll see what's written on the page, look at a spreadsheet and you'll see rows and columns, look at a movie and it will start playing. All this without having to open the program associated with that file.

While Quick Look is visible, click a different file and Quick Look will display that file instead. Switch Finder windows (you can have a gazillion Finder windows open at a time) and Quick Look will display the item in the current window. You can even preview more than one file at a time with Quick Look: select multiple files and arrows will appear at the top of the Quick Look window that you can use to flip through previews of all the files you selected.

Make an alias

There are times you want access to a file or folder without having to burrow through directories to get at it. Some people's first inclination is to move the item to a more accessible location, but the best solution is to make an alias. An alias acts just like the regular file or folder but it points to the original: put something in a folder alias and it ends up in the original (target) folder. Delete the alias and the item it refers to is unaffected.

You can spot an alias by a curved arrow in the lower-left corner of its icon. To create an alias, select a file in the Finder and then choose File→Make Alias (or press ⌘-L). Then simply drag the alias to where you want it to be.

Duplicate files and folders

If you want a copy of a file or folder, click the item in the Finder and then select File→Duplicate (or press ⌘-D), and Lion will generate a brand-new copy of that item with the word "copy" appended to its name. Your original item will remain untouched while you hack away at the copy.

Copy files to a new location on the same disk

When you drag files from one spot to another on the same disk, Mac OS X moves those files to the new location without making a copy. To *copy* files to another location on the same disk instead, hold Option while you drag the files to the new location. Once you release the mouse button, the original file(s) stay put, and you get a copy in the destination location.

Conversely, when you drag files from one disk to another, Mac OS X *copies* them. To make it move them instead, you have to hold down the ⌘ key while you drag.

Eject a drive or disk

If you've got external drives hooked to your Mac, at some point you'll want to eject them. Just yanking the drive out is a bad idea; if data is still being written to the drive, you might lose it.

You have a few ways of ejecting drives and disks. The classic way of ejecting a drive on a Mac is to drag it to the Trash (when you do, the Trash's icon changes to an Eject icon). If you've got a Finder window open, you can also eject it directly from the sidebar—simply click the ⏏ next to the drive's icon. If a drive won't eject, Lion will tell you which application is using files on that drive (and preventing you from ejecting it).

If you want to remount a drive (use the drive after you've ejected it) that you left plugged in, you can either remount it with Disk Utility (*/Applications/Utilities/Disk Utility*) or simply disconnect the drive from your Mac and then reconnect it.

Reformat a disk

If you've got a new disk, it might not be in the right format. Most flash drives and many pocket drives come formatted as FAT32 disks, but some arrive unformatted. Your Mac prefers the Mac OS Extended (Journaled) filesystem, and if you don't need to share files with another operating system (such as Windows), this format is your best choice. To erase the drive and format it as Mac OS Extended (Journaled), head to */Applications/Utilities/Disk Utility*. Select the disk you want to reformat from the list on the left side of Disk Utility, click the Erase tab and select the format you want, and then click Erase. Remember: formatting erases all the information on the disk.

Compress files and folders

If you're going to burn a bunch of data to a disk or if you want to minimize upload times, you can compress files and folders. Lion gives you an easy way to pull this off: right-click or Control-click a file, and then select Compress from the pop-up menu, and Lion will create a copy of that item with the same name, but with the suffix *.zip* appended. The amount of space this saves depends on the type of file: compressing a QuickTime movie (*.mov*) doesn't save as much space as compressing a folder full of text files does, for example.

Duplicating Optical Disks

DVDs and CDs are getting less popular for sharing files because of the availability of cheap flash drives, but they're still common enough that you might need to make backup copies of important data stored on a CD or DVD. If you have a desktop Mac, you could install two DVD drives and copy DVDs and CDs disk-to-disk, but that option's only available on high-end Macs (although you could use an external USB drive with other Macs). No worries, though; with Disk Utility, you can easily duplicate that DVD or CD and burn it to a different disk.

Fire up Disk Utility (*/Applications/Utilities/Disk Utility*) and then select the CD or DVD you want to copy from the list of available disks. Next, click the New Image button at the top of the window, choose "DVD/CD master" from the Image Format pop-up menu, and choose a location with sufficient disk space from the Where pop-up menu. Click Save and Lion makes an image (a special type of copy) of the DVD.

Once the copying operation is complete, you'll have a perfect copy of the DVD or CD on your drive. To burn that copy onto a blank CD or DVD, select the disk image from the list on the left side of Disk Utility (if it's not there, drag the disk image from the Finder into the list), then click the Burn button and insert a blank disk when prompted. (Alas, this approach won't work for copy-protected software or movies.)

The Dock

The Dock is a key aspect of Mac OS X. It contains shortcuts to frequently used applications, folders, and documents, and it shows you which applications are running by placing a blue dot under each one. (A lot of people detest the blue dots, and in Lion you get the option to turn them off: just head to System Preferences→Dock and then uncheck the box next to "Show indicator lights for open applications.") A typical Dock is shown in Figure 3-17.

Figure 3-17. A typical Dock

You can use the Dock to switch between active applications; just click the Dock icon of the one you want to switch to and that will become the frontmost application. When an application is starting up, its Dock icon will bounce so you can tell that it's loading. If an already-running application's icon begins bouncing, that's the Dock's way of telling you the application wants your attention.

The Finder is on the far left side of the Dock and is always running. To the right of that, you'll see application icons, a divider, the Documents stack, the Downloads stack, any minimized windows, and the Trash.

NOTE

In Snow Leopard, the Dock featured an Applications stack, too. (If you updated from Snow Leopard to Lion, you'll still see this stack in the Dock.) But with the addition of Launchpad, the Applications stack has become redundant. If you want that stack back, just drag your Applications folder onto the Dock.

Since the Dock is conveniently located, it is a natural way of opening your most-used applications and documents. The obvious question is how do you add items to the Dock? The process is simple: just locate the application or document you want to add and drag it onto the Dock. Keep in mind, though, that you can only put applications on the left side of the Dock's divider and you can only put documents on the right side of the divider. (Even if you haven't placed an application or document in the Dock, it will appear there as long as it's running or open.) Note that adding items to the Dock doesn't move or change the original item, and removing items from the Dock doesn't delete them from your Mac.

You can arrange items in the Dock by dragging them into the order you want. (Dragging a running application that's not already in the Dock will add it.)

NOTE

If you want to try to force a particular document to open in a specific application, drag the file onto the desired application's icon in the Finder or Dock, and that application will generally try to open the file. However, some applications respond differently: dragging something onto the Mail icon, for example, attaches it to a new message.

Once your Dock is fully loaded with applications and documents, it can get a little overwhelming. If you forget what that minimized window is for or what application will start if you click a certain icon, the Dock can help you out. Simply hover your cursor over the Dock item in question and a text bubble will pop up with info about that item, as shown in Figure 3-18.

Figure 3-18. Forget what application an icon is for? The Dock has your answer!

Removing items from the Dock is easy. You can drag the unwanted item off of the Dock, drag it onto the Trash icon, or right-click or Control-click the item in question and, in the pop-up menu that appears, select "Remove from Dock."

Dock Exposé

Lion has replaced Exposé with Mission Control, but you can still use Exposé for applications. The way you do this is really slick: pick any running application, click and hold its icon in the Dock, and then select Show All Windows in the pop-up menu that appears. You then see something like Figure 3-19.

Figure 3-19. Safari's open and minimized windows displayed in Dock Exposé

When you invoke Dock Exposé, you'll see all the selected application's open windows. Any minimized windows show up as small versions below a subtle dividing line. Click any window to bring it to the front.

The pop-up menu that appears when you click and hold an application's Dock icon also lets you quit or hide the selected application. The menu also includes an Options submenu to let you keep the application in the Dock, set it to open each time you log into the computer, or show it in the Finder.

Dock menus

Every item in the Dock also has a Dock menu. To access this menu, right-click or Control-click the icon. What shows up in the menu depends on what you click and, in the case of applications, whether it's running and what it's doing. Application Dock menus typically include relevant commands. For example, if you're currently playing a song, iTunes's Dock menu lets you mute your computer, skip and rate songs, and so forth. All applications' Dock menus include these options:

- Options→Keep in Dock or Remove from Dock, depending on current setting
- Options→Open at Login (saves you a trip to the Users & Groups preference pane)
- Options→Show in Finder (reveals where the application resides on your Mac)
- Hide (hides all the application's windows; equivalent to pressing ⌘-H)
- Quit (closes the application; you'll be warned if there are any unsaved changes)

The Dock menus for stacks (such as the Documents or Downloads stack) offer a different set of choices:

- Sort by options (Name, Date Added, Date Modified, Date Created, Kind)
- Display as (Folder or Stack)
- View content as (Fan, Grid, List, Automatic)
- Options (Remove from Dock or Show in Finder)
- Open [stack name]

Stack view options

Those folders or jumbled icons (depending on how your preferences are set—jumbled icons is the default) on the right side of your Dock are called stacks. You can choose which view to use for each stack by opening its Dock menu (the previous section explains how). Here are your options:

Fan View

> This is the default view of a stack. If you click a stack that's set to this view, it'll fan out, making it easy to choose the item you're looking for, as shown in Figure 3-20. Fan View is nice when there aren't a lot of items in a stack; it's less helpful when there are more than a dozen or so items. If you use the arrow keys to select items in the stack, a blue highlight appears behind the current item; hit Return to open it.

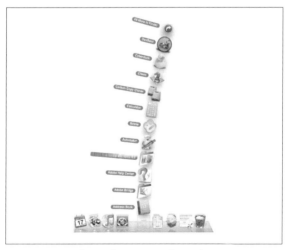

Figure 3-20. Exploring the contents of a stack in Fan View

Grid View

> In Grid View (Figure 3-21), you get to browse by icon, and you can use the arrow keys to highlight an item. If that

Figure 3-21. The excellent Grid View

item is an application or document, hitting the Return key starts the application or opens the document. If the selected item is a folder, hitting Return opens *another* Grid View window that displays the folder's contents.

List View

List View (Figure 3-22) got a bit of an upgrade in Lion. Instead of the boring list on a white background, your options are now displayed as a list on the same background used by Grid View. Even with the new background, List View is a bit pedestrian compared to Fan View or Grid View, but that doesn't mean it is useless. You can scroll through the list using the ↑ and ↓ keys, and when you run across a folder, pressing the → key opens a submenu with the enclosed items.

Automatic View

If you don't feel like fine-tuning the way a stack is displayed, you can let Lion pick a view for you based on the stack's contents. To get Lion to make this difficult

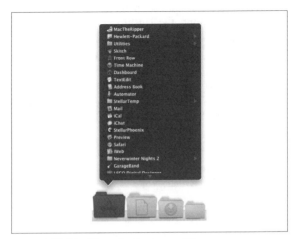

Figure 3-22. List View—boring but useful

decision for you, right-click or Control-click the stack and then choose Automatic from the "View content as" section of the pop-up menu.

Trash

It doesn't matter if you've got a relatively tiny SSD drive in a MacBook Air or 4 terabytes of hard disk space in a fully tricked-out Mac Pro. Sooner or later, you're going to want to get rid of some files either because your drive(s) are feeling cramped or because you just don't want the data around anymore. To get rid of something that's on your Mac, you'll need to use the Trash.

The Trash is located on the right end of the Dock (or, if you've moved the Dock to the left or right of your screen, it's on the bottom). To banish files from your Mac, select them and then drag them from the Finder to the Trash (or press ⌘-Delete).

When the Trash has something in it (whether it's one item or a million), its icon changes from an empty mesh trash can to a can stuffed with paper. This lets you know that the files you've moved to the Trash are still there, and that you can retrieve them (until you empty the Trash).

Open the Trash by clicking its Dock icon. (You can view the items in the Trash with the Finder, but you won't be able to actually open a file that's in the Trash; attempting to do so will result in an error message.) If you find something in the Trash that shouldn't be there, you can either drag it out of the Trash or click File→Put Back to send it back to where it was originally.

To *permanently* delete items in the Trash, right-click or Control-click the Trash's Dock icon and choose Empty Trash, or open the Finder and either choose Finder→Empty Trash or press Shift-⌘-Delete.

Note that emptying the Trash doesn't completely remove all traces of the files you deleted. Those files can be recovered with third-party drive-recovery utilities, at least until the disk space they previously occupied has been written over with new data. To make it harder for people to recover deleted data, in the Finder, choose Finder→Secure Empty Trash. This command overwrites the deleted files multiple times.

If you work with a lot of sensitive files, you can tell the Trash to *always* write over files you delete by going to the Finder's preferences (Finder→Preferences or ⌘-, while in the Finder) and, on the Advanced tab, checking the box next to "Empty Trash securely." You probably want to leave the "Show warning before emptying the Trash" option checked because, once you securely empty the Trash, you're not getting that data back.

Dock preferences

Here are a few quick and easy changes you can make without invoking the Dock's preference pane. If you right-click or Control-click the divider between the two parts of the Dock (it looks like a dashed line), you'll get the pop-up menu shown in Figure 3-23. This menu lets you choose whether to automatically hide the Dock when you're not using it, change the magnification of icons in the Dock, change the Dock's location, change the animation OS X uses when you minimize windows, and open the Dock's preferences.

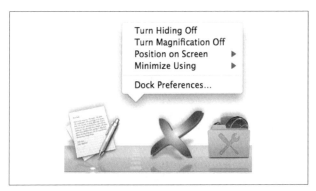

Figure 3-23. A quick way to make Dock adjustments

You can change the size of the Dock by dragging up or down over the dashed dividing line to increase or decrease the size of the Dock, respectively.

The Application Switcher

The Dock is the most obvious way to switch between applications while they're running, and Mission Control is probably the niftiest way, but Lion gives you a third way to flip between your open apps. The aptly named Application Switcher (Figure 3-24) lets you switch applications without taking your hands off the keyboard, a huge timesaver if you find yourself change programs often. To use it, just hit ⌘-Tab.

Figure 3-24. Hands on the keyboard and you're still switching applications!

Holding the ⌘ key while repeatedly hitting the Tab key cycles through the open applications from left to right (use Shift-Tab instead to go from right to left), and then wraps around to the first application on the left again. Alternatively, you can press ⌘-Tab and then, while still holding down ⌘, use the ← and → keys to move between applications. When the application you want to switch to has a white border around it, release the keys and that program will come to the front.

Standard Window Controls

All windows in Mac OS X share some characteristics, shown in Figure 3-25. Knowing what they do will help you be much more productive when using Lion.

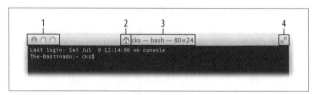

Figure 3-25. Lion's standard window controls, which live on the title bar

Here's what these controls do:

1. The red button closes the window. If you hover your cursor over this dot, you'll see an × or—if there are unsaved changes to the current document—a dark-red dot inside it. The yellow button minimizes a window; put your cursor over this dot and you see a –. The green button maximizes the window, and displays a + when you point to it.

2. This is called the proxy icon. Drag it to create an alias of the current file, or Option-drag it to copy the current file.

3. The name of the current file.

4. If the application you're using can go full screen, you'll see these arrows. See the section "Full-Screen Applications" on page 5 for details.

The following table lists some keyboard shortcuts that are useful for working with windows.

Action	Key command
Open a new window	⌘-O
Close the active window	⌘-W
Minimize the active window	⌘-M
Minimize all windows for the frontmost application	Option-⌘-M
Cycle through an application's windows	⌘-`

NOTE

Not every key combination is universal. For example, some applications use ⌘-M for something other than minimizing the active window.

Files and Folders

As you already know, folders are where you keep files. But Mac OS X also includes two special kinds of folders: the Burn folder and the Smart folder.

Regular Folders

Your Mac comes preloaded with some folders that are appropriate for commonly saved files (documents, pictures, music, and so on), but you'll also want to make your own folders. For example, you might make a subfolder for spreadsheets within the Documents folder, or put a folder on your desktop where you can toss files that end up on the desktop. To create a regular folder in the Finder, you can either choose File→New Folder

(Shift-⌘-N), or right-click or Control-click a blank spot in a folder and then choose New Folder from the Context menu shown in Figure 3-26.

Figure 3-26. Creating a new folder via the Context menu

Mac OS X names new folders "untitled folder," and it iterates this name if you create a series of folders without renaming them after you create each one, so you end up with untitled folder, untitled folder 1, untitled folder 2, and so on. To change a folder's name, click the folder once and then press Return or click the folder's title. The area surrounding the title gets highlighted and you can type the new name. When you're done, hit Return to make the name stick (until you change it again).

Burn Folders

Creating a Burn folder is the easiest way to get files or folders from your Mac onto an optical disk (a CD or DVD). To do so, go to the Finder and select File→New Burn Folder. A new folder with a radiation symbol in it will show up in the current folder. (If you've made filename extensions visible—see "Finder preferences" on page 63—you'll notice that folder's suffix is *.fpbf*.)

Be sure to give this folder a nice, descriptive name like *discoin-ferno*. Then you can start tossing any files you want burned onto the disk into that folder.

The files aren't actually being moved to the Burn folder; Lion is just creating aliases that point to them. When the time comes to burn the data, Mac OS X will burn the original file(s). Since the files are aliased, if you decide you want to get rid of the Burn folder without burning the data, you can toss the folder into the Trash. The original items will remain untouched.

Once you're ready to burn the data, open the Burn folder and then click the Burn button in its upper-right corner. Insert a disk when prompted, and Lion takes care of the rest.

Smart Folders

There are Smart folders all over your Mac: in iTunes, Mail, and lots of other places. Smart folders are actually Spotlight search results, but you can browse them just like regular folders.

To create your own Smart folders, head to the Finder and choose File→New Smart Folder or press Option-⌘-N. In the Search box of the new window that appears, type in text describing what you want to find and Lion will fill the folder with items that meet your criteria.

Lion is smarter about creating Smart folders than its predecessors. As you type, Lion displays suggestions for refining your search. Say you want an easy way to manage all your Word files. Start typing ".doc" in the Search box, and Lion will make handy suggestions like the ones shown in Figure 3-27. Select "Word Document" under Kinds and all your Word documents will appear in the Smart folder.

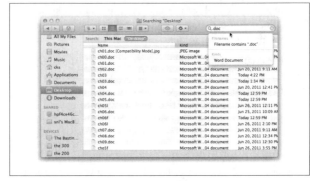

Figure 3-27. Lion knows what you're looking for

If the results aren't quite what you want, you can further refine your search by clicking the + button below the Search box. You can adjust the search by hitting the + button. When you do, you'll see a new set of criteria and another + button that you can click to add another set of criteria. You can keep adding more criteria until your search is *just* the way you want it (Figure 3-28).

Figure 3-28. A search so refined it returns no results

Want to save your search? No problem—click the Save button to save your search as a Smart folder. You'll get to name it, choose where to save it, and, if you wish, add it to the sidebar.

There are more great things about Smart folders. The results of your search don't change where anything is actually stored on your Mac, but you can act as if all the files reside in the Smart folder you just created. That means that, even though the files in it could be scattered across a hundred folders on your Mac, you can move, copy, and delete them just as if they all resided in the Smart folder. (If you delete a file from a Smart folder, you'll also delete that file from your Mac.)

Don't worry about your Smart folders slowing down your Mac or not displaying changes immediately. Smart folders are constantly updated, so when you add a new file that fits the Smart folder's criteria, the file will show up in the Smart folder right away.

Nonessential (but Useful) Mac OS X Features

Some features of Lion are really useful but not strictly required for day-to-day use. For example, some people never use Dashboard, while others can't get by without it. Spotlight is fantastic for searching your Mac, but some folks never search their Macs because they have insanely good organizational skills. Spaces can make that 13-inch laptop screen seem much bigger. And Mission Control lets you see everything on your desktop (and more) at the same time—a lifesaver for those who work with multiple windows. If you're interested in one or more of these features, this is the place to look.

The Dashboard

That speedometer-like icon in your Dock launches Dashboard, an environment where mini-applications (called widgets) run. Click the icon, use a gesture, or use the keyboard shortcut (it's F4 on most Macs that can run Lion). If you don't have the F4 shortcut on your keyboard, you can use the Keyboard preference pane to add a shortcut or see what the shortcut is. Once you invoke Dashboard, your Desktop will slide away. In Snow Leopard, Dashboard floated over your desktop with a translucent background, but in Lion, Dashboard gets a solid background to make the desktop less distracting.

Once Dashboard is up and running, the widgets on it will go about doing whatever they're supposed to do (reporting on the weather, displaying a calendar, and so on). To get back to your desktop, click the arrow in the bottom right of the Dashboard or press the Dashboard key again.

Lion comes with several widgets built in, but only a few will already be in the Dashboard by default: calculator, weather, calendar, and clock widgets. Click the + button at the Dashboard's lower left to add any of these:

Address Book
> Lets you search your Address Book from the Dashboard.

Calculator
> This is just a basic calculator; it's much less powerful than the Calculator application built into Mac OS X. If you want a more powerful widgetified calculator, you can find one at Apple's widget repository (*http://www.apple.com/ downloads/dashboard*).

Dictionary
> This gives you the same information as the Mac OS X Dictionary application (though without the Wikipedia browsing capabilities). You can use this widget as a dictionary, a thesaurus, or an Apple help interface.

ESPN
> Fetches scores and news about your favorite teams.

Flight Tracker
> Lets you track flights in real time. If your spouse or roommate is returning from a trip, you can see how long you have left to clean up the house.

iCal
> Lets you view iCal events in convenient widget form.

Movies
> Keeps you up to date on the movies playing in your area. Initially, it just cycles through the posters of currently

playing movies, but when you click on it, it'll display showtimes and theaters.

Ski Report

Like to ski? This widget keeps you updated on the conditions at your favorite slopes.

Stickies

This is the Dashboard version of Stickies (see "Stickies" on page 175).

Stocks

Got some stocks? Track the roller-coaster ride of investing in the market with this widget.

Tile Game

If you had a pre–OS X Mac, you might remember the game Tile that came as a desk accessory. This is a widgetized version of it. Instead of a picture of the Apple logo, you get to unscramble a picture of a big cat. The tile-scrambling animation is worth watching, even if you never actually play with this widget.

Translation

Translate a word or phrase from one language to another. The shorter the phrase, the more accurate the translation.

Unit Converter

Shouldn't everyone be using SI units by now? Well, probably, but they don't. With this widget, you can discover how many liters there are in an imperial gallon.

Weather

Track the upcoming weather with this widget. You only get to choose one city to track, so if you want to know the weather in more than one place when using Dashboard, you'll need to have multiple Weather widgets running.

Web Clip

Web Clip lets you create your own widgets! See "Making your own widgets" on page 91 to learn how.

World Clock
> If you're using Dashboard all the time and you don't have a watch or you want to know the time in Geneva while you're in San Francisco, this widget has you covered.

Personalizing widgets

You can't personalize every widget, but you have to personalize some (like the Weather widget) to make them useful. To set a widget's preferences, look for an *i* somewhere on the widget (usually, but not always, in the lower-right corner of the widget; you may have to put your cursor over the widget to make it appear).

Adding and removing widgets

In the lower-left corner of the Dashboard, you'll see a + inside a circle. Clicking this reveals a line of available widgets at the bottom of the screen. If you see a widget you want to add, just drag it to the location where you want it to live on the Dashboard. You can overlap widgets and have multiple instances of the same widget, so if you're not careful, it can quickly get confusing.

The easiest way to delete a widget from your Dashboard (but not from your Mac) is to hold the Option key, hover your cursor over the widget, and then click the × that appears in the widget's upper-left corner. If you change your mind, you can simply add that widget again later. If you want to get rid of a widget forever, use Widget Manager.

Widget Manager lets you exert more control over widgets. To use it, click the + in the lower left of the Dashboard, and then click the Manage Widgets button that appears. A widget (of course) pops up, giving you the chance to disable individual widgets by unchecking the boxes next to them. A disabled widget won't be available from the widget bar until you re-enable it with Widget Manager. Third-party widgets (discussed next) get a deletion circle next to them; if you click the –, you'll be asked if you want to move the widget to the Trash.

Getting more widgets

The widgets Apple includes are great, but there's a whole world of other widgets out there. To find more, the best place to go is Apple's index of widgets: *http://www.apple.com/downloads/dashboard.* (If you have Widget Manager up, you can click the More Widgets button to zip straight to this site.) You'll be amazed at the number of available widgets. Most are free, but some will set you back a few bucks.

Making your own widgets

There are a ton of widgets available for download, but there's still a chance that the widget you desire doesn't exist. You could write your own widget to rectify the situation—after all, widgets are just snippets of code—or you could take the easy way out and create one using a Web Clip. For example, imagine you wrote a book and want to keep tabs on its sales ranking at Amazon. You could go to Amazon every day and scroll down to the ranking, but that takes too much effort. Why not create your own Web Clip widget to take care of the data retrieval for you?

Here's how: Open Safari and find the information you want your Web Clip to retrieve. Then choose File→"Open in Dashboard" and a white box will appear. Drag this box so that it surrounds the information you want to keep constantly updated with. Then click the Add button or hit Return and your new widget will show up in Dashboard. (Some pages work better than others, so you might need to experiment a bit.)

Searching with Spotlight

Using Spotlight is easy: Simply click the magnifying glass icon in the upper-right corner of your screen and start typing the name of the item you're looking for.

In Snow Leopard, Spotlight only let you search through the files on your computer. But in Lion, you can also use the new and improved version of Spotlight to search the web or Wikipedia, as shown in Figure 3-29. (The results will open with OS X's Dictionary application.).

Searching the Internet and Wikipedia aren't the only upgrades to Spotlight in Lion. You also get Quick Look previews: just highlight the most promising-looking result and Quick Look will give you a detailed look at the file or web page. Plus, you can drag and drop things directly from Spotlight. Found that GarageBand file you want to send to your pal? Drag it right to AirDrop (see "AirDrop" on page 11) to make the process quick and painless.

When it's searching your computer, Spotlight works by indexing (making a list of) all the files on your Mac according to the files' *metadata* and contents. So if you type "Lake Monsters Stole My Thursday" into a document, that bit of data will be available to Spotlight. The moment you type "lake monsters stole" into Spotlight's search field, you'll see a list of matching files. By the time you've typed the entire string into Spotlight, the document you typed it into will be the top result.

Figure 3-29. Choose where you want your results to come from

About Metadata

Metadata is information about a file. This includes obvious things like the date it was created and its file type, as well as a lot of unexpected information. An image's metadata, for example, contains information about its size, pixel count, and so on. Spotlight is smart enough to realize that when you're searching, you're most likely searching for a particular file's name or contents, as opposed to more esoteric metadata. So, while Spotlight indexes everything (unless you tell it not to—see "Controlling what Spotlight indexes" on page 94), it puts results like documents and folders higher on its lists of results than more obscure matches (unless you change the order of its results—see "Controlling the results Spotlight displays" on page 93). That way, you won't be burdened by information overload when performing a Spotlight search.

Changing the order of Spotlight's results

You can adjust how Spotlight arranges its results either by choosing →System Preferences→Spotlight→Search Results or clicking Spotlight Preferences at the bottom of any list of Spotlight search results. In the window that appears, drag the categories into your preferred order.

Controlling the results Spotlight displays

If you don't want your Spotlight search results cluttered with stuff you're not interested in, go to System Preferences→Spotlight→Search Results and uncheck the boxes next to any categories you find less than compelling. Be aware that not returning results from certain categories doesn't mean those files aren't indexed; read on to learn how to control *what* Spotlight indexes.

Controlling what Spotlight indexes

There are some things you just don't want indexed: your plans for world domination, your Pog value spreadsheet, and so forth. To keep the things you want private out of Spotlight's index, go to System Preferences→Spotlight→Privacy. Clicking the + button brings up a file-browsing window where you can select things you want to keep Spotlight from indexing. You can exclude folders or entire disks. Unfortunately, you can't exclude a single file, so if you're trying to keep just one file out of the index, you either have to exclude the folder it's in (along with all of the folder's other contents) or move it into its own folder and exclude that.

Managing File Info

As you learned above, Spotlight works by indexing metadata. What if you want to add some metadata so Spotlight can find files or folders with greater precision? The Info window is your key to adding metadata (and changing other things, too). To open an item's Info window, select the item in the Finder and then either select File→Get Info or press ⌘-I. The window that appears will look something like Figure 3-30.

This window has several subsections.

Spotlight comments

Here's where you can add terms for Spotlight to use. Anything you type here will be indexed by Spotlight and used when it searches.

General

This section includes pertinent data about the file (if this section is collapsed, click the disclosure triangle next to "General"). If you check the "Stationery pad" box (which only appears when applicable), the file turns into a read-only file, meaning you can look at it and save it as a new file, but you can't save it with the same name as the Stationery pad; this

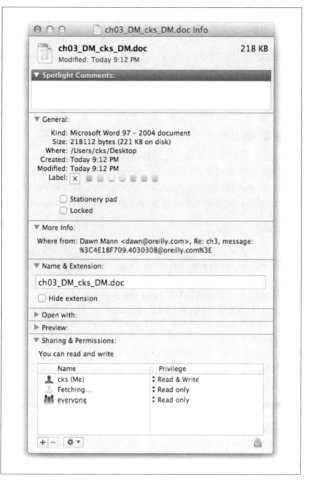

Figure 3-30. Get Info is a very useful window

effectively turns the file into a template. Checking the Lock box locks the file. A locked file is much like a Stationery pad, except you can't easily throw it away. You'll get warnings when you move a locked file to the Trash, and again when you go to empty the Trash.

More Info

Clicking the More Info disclosure triangle reveals where the file originated if it wasn't created on your Mac. (The file shown in Figure 3-30 happens to be the chapter you're reading.)

Name & Extension

This section lets you rename the item and hide its extension (by checking the box). You can also change the extension, but that will (likely) change which program opens the file. If you change the extension, you'll get a warning from Mac OS X.

Open with

This section is surprisingly powerful. You can choose the application you want to open this particular file with, or you can change what programs open any file with the same extension by clicking Change All. Clicking the pop-up menu will reveal suggested choices, but if you don't want to trust Mac OS X's advice, you can select Other to force a different application to open that file.

Preview

This section shows the same preview of the file that you'd see when using the Finder.

Sharing & Permissions

This is where you can fine-tune access to the file. The options you're first presented with differ depending on the file, but generally concern your account, an admin, and everyone. Those are usually enough, but if you *really* want to control who can and can't mess with a particular file, click the + button to bring up even more options, as shown in Figure 3-31.

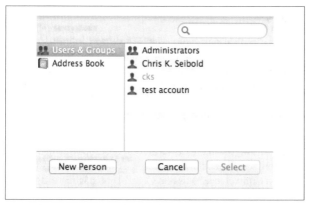

Figure 3-31. Fine-tuning who can share a file

In the window that appears, you can grant access to specific individuals. Note that adding someone new (from your Address Book, for instance) will bring up a dialog box where you can set a password for the item, and will add a Sharing account to your Mac for that person. Adding a new group of people will add a new Group account.

Finally, if you've made a bunch of changes to sharing and then thought better of it, you can click the gear icon and then undo what you have wrought by selecting "Revert changes."

NOTE

The Sharing & Permissions section also includes a lock icon. If you're logged in as a Standard user, you can click it to unlock restricted features, such as the Change All button in the "Open with" section. However, you'll need the username and password of an administrative user to make changes.

Spaces

During a typical day, your Mac's desktop can get cluttered. You might have a NeoOffice window open, an iTunes window floating about, a Safari window for browsing the Web, and an iMovie window open while you make some last minute edits to your vacation movie. You're thinking, "Thank goodness for the Application Switcher," but there's a better (and complementary) solution: Spaces.

Spaces allow you to create additional desktops devoted to application windows. Sound great? Get started by heading to Mission Control (see "Mission Control" on page 6) and adding desktop spaces for all your different workflows (up to 16).

CHAPTER 4

Troubleshooting Mac OS X

Mac OS X is a robust operating system; while problems are rare, they do show up from time to time. Since these problems always seem to present themselves at the worst possible moment, it helps if you know the best ways to troubleshoot them. Troubleshooting is what this chapter is about, and it's a great reason to keep this book in your pocket!

Common Problems

There are a lot of things that can go wrong with your Mac: Hardware problems, software glitches, and configuration issues can happen at any moment. Most of the problems you'll encounter can be easily addressed or diagnosed by following the steps in this chapter. If the information here doesn't resolve things, you could have a unique issue, in which case a trip to the Apple Store or a call to Apple is in order.

NOTE

You can find a complete list of technical support numbers for Apple at *http://www.apple.com/support/contact/phone_contacts.html*. In the United States, the number is 1-800-275-2273.

Misbehaving Applications

One of the most common problems on a Mac is an application that isn't behaving as expected. This problem comes in many forms: an application that unexpectedly quits repeatedly, simply stops responding, or just doesn't perform the way it normally does. This section suggests ways to resolve all these issues and more.

An application stops responding

Occasionally, an application will simply stop reacting to anything. Your mouse or trackpad will still work, and other programs will be fine, but if you want to use the troublesome program all you'll get is a spinning beach-ball cursor (instead of the mouse pointer) and you'll have no way to input anything.

Don't panic—there's an easy fix. Simply right-click or Control-click the stalled application's icon in the Dock to bring up its Dock menu (Figure 4-1). If you see "Application Not Responding" in faint text at the top of the menu, you'll also see a Force Quit option. Select Force Quit and Mac OS X will kill the program.

You may also need another way to kill applications, because occasionally a program can become unresponsive without Mac OS X realizing that the program is in peril. For these times, launch the Force Quit Applications dialog box either by selecting ⌘→Force Quit or using the key combo Option-⌘-Esc. You can also try holding down Shift as you click the ⌘ menu, then select Force Quit [application name] to kill the frontmost application.

There's some good news when it comes to force-quitting applications in Lion. In previous versions of OS X, any changes you made between the last time you saved a document and the moment the application started misbehaving were gone forever. But Lion includes Auto Save, a new feature that automatically saves your work as you go. So if you're forced to quit

Figure 4-1. When an application isn't playing nicely, Force Quit is your best option

an application, Lion preserves the work you've done since the last time you saved.

WARNING

For the time being, "Save early, save often" is still good advice, since Lion's Auto Save feature only works with applications specifically built with Auto Save in mind. That means that work you do in apps designed for Lion will be saved, but applications that haven't been updated for Lion *won't* automatically save your work.

The Finder stops responding

The Finder is just another program, so it can get hung up, too. If that happens, either head to →Force Quit or use the key combination ⌘-Option-Esc. If nothing happens, try clicking the Dock or some other application first, and *then* use the menu or ⌘-Option-Esc to invoke the Force Quit dialog box.

Force quitting greedy processes

If you suspect something is eating up too much processor time or too many system resources (because your Mac is running really slowly, say, or the fans are running at full speed for no obvious reason), Force Quit won't help you figure out which application is hogging all the resources. Instead, open Activity Monitor (Applications→Utilities→Activity Monitor), click its CPU tab, and then look for any processes that are using a lot of CPU resources for more than a few seconds. (Safari and its helper applications occasionally do this, particularly with runaway Flash or JavaScript code.) When you identify a suspect, single-click the renegade process's name and then click the big red Quit Process button in the upper-left corner of the Activity Monitor window (you can't miss it—it's shaped like a stop sign).

USB device problems

It seems like computers never have enough USB ports, so most of us end up using USB hubs (or keyboards that have extra USB ports). Then we plug some fantastic new USB device into the hub—and it doesn't work. In fact, if you dig through System Information (it's in the */Applications/Utilities* folder) and look at the USB Device Tree (click USB in the list on the left), the hub shows up, but not the device.

Often the problem is that the device requires a *powered* USB port and you're using an unpowered hub (or you've maxed out the power capabilities of the hub or port). Switching to a powered hub might fix the problem, but it isn't guaranteed. What works most often is plugging the device directly into your Mac, which means you'll need to shuffle your various USB devices around. If any of them can run off of their own external power supply rather than taking power from the USB port, that may help as well (sometimes these power supplies are sold separately; check with the device's manufacturer).

The second method of attacking USB device problems is a little more involved. First, shut down your Mac and unplug all the USB devices (even the ones that use external power supplies). Reboot your Mac, and then plug them back in one at a time while watching at the USB Device Tree (it's updated quickly so you'll see each device appear as it's plugged in) to see which device isn't playing nicely with others.

Sometimes going through this process results in all of the devices suddenly working. But if you figure out that only a certain device isn't working, the fix may be to install a new driver for it. Check the manufacturer's website for updates.

NOTE

Some USB devices, such as a GPS unit or other gadget that behaves like a serial port, rely on a chipset from a different manufacturer than the one that makes the device. Two common sources of USB-serial devices are Prolific (*http://www.prolific.com.tw/eng/Download.asp*) and FTDI (*http://www.ftdichip.com/FTDrivers.htm*).

Battery problems

MacBook users are faced with a problem that desktop users don't have to worry about: the battery. The goal of most Apple batteries is to still provide 80% of the original charge capacity after a certain number of cycles (charges and discharges). The number of cycles varies depending on your machine. For Lion-capable MacBooks, the cycle count is either 750 or 1000 cycles (depending on the model). If you notice your battery isn't holding a charge for as long as it used to, the first thing to do is launch System Information (Applications→Utilities→System Information) and then click Power in the list on the left; see Figure 4-2.

The Battery Information list includes your battery's full charge capacity, how many cycles it's been through, and its condition. If the condition is listed as Replace Soon or something equally ominous, it's likely time to think about getting a new battery. If the cycle count is low but the battery is *still* running out of juice prematurely, here are a couple of things you can try:

Calibrate the battery

Inside every MacBook battery is a microcontroller that tells your computer how long the battery is going to last until it runs out of juice. Over time, this estimation can get farther and farther from real-world performance. To get the computer and the microcontroller on the same page, you need to recalibrate the battery from time to time. To do so, fully charge the battery and then keep your computer plugged into the power adapter for two more

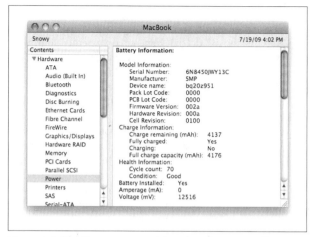

Figure 4-2. The Power section of System Information tells you all about your battery

hours. Next, unplug the power adapter and fully drain the battery. When a warning pops up alerting you that the battery is running dangerously low, save your work and keep on trucking until your computer automatically goes to sleep. Then let the computer sleep for more than five hours to make sure every drop of power is gone. Finally, plug in the power adapter and let your computer fully charge. The battery indicator should now be successfully recalibrated.

NOTE

If your MacBook has an internal battery, Apple recommends *not* calibrating the battery because these internal batteries should only be serviced by an authorized repair center.

Reset the SMC

SMC is short for the System Management Controller, a chip that's responsible for hard drive spin-down, sleep and wake, and backlighting. A malfunctioning SMC can prevent the battery from charging, so you need to reset the SMC. How you do that depends on whether your MacBook has an internal or external battery. If it has an external battery, shut it down, unplug the power adapter from the wall and the computer, and then remove the battery. Next, press the power button for five seconds. After that, replace the battery, plug in the power adapter, and then restart the computer. If your MacBook has an internal battery, shut the computer down and plug it into an adapter that is getting power. On the left side of the keyboard, hold down Left Shift-Control-Option and then press the power button. Keep these buttons depressed (including the power button) for five seconds and then release them all simultaneously. Pat yourself on the back for pulling off an impressive feat of manual dexterity and then press the power button to restart the computer.

If those remedies don't restore your battery, it's likely time for a trip to your local Apple Store or authorized repair center. If your computer is under warranty and your cycle count is low, Apple will probably replace the battery. If your cycle count is over the recommended number and the performance degradation is within expectations, you'll probably need to have the battery replaced or live with the reduced (and ever-shrinking) battery capacity.

NOTE

Like many computer makers, Apple has had its share of battery recalls, both for safety and performance reasons. So check with Apple to see if your battery is under recall. If so, it's likely that Apple will replace the battery even if your computer is out of warranty.

Display problems

Most Macs come with a built-in display that doesn't require special configuration, so display problems are uncommon. When they do happen, they're often caused by user error. The fix, while usually easy, isn't readily apparent. Here are some things to try:

Fuzzy/tiny display

If your display is fuzzy or everything is suddenly bigger than you remember, it's possible that someone changed the display's resolution (on some systems, this may also manifest itself as a small screen with black bars around its edges). Head to Applications→System Preferences→Displays and look for the monitor's native resolution (on Macs with built-in displays, this is usually the highest resolution available at the top of the list). Once you select the optimal resolution, things should look normal again.

Your display moves with your mouse

I've received several panicked calls and emails about this issue. The weird thing is that it always happens when children under five are on your lap while you're using your computer. Is there some kind of kid detector in your Mac that causes this? Of course not. Your kid just pressed some keys while you were working. (If you don't have kids or lap cats, then it was probably you.)

There are a couple of key combinations that will cause your Mac to zoom the screen. The most common is holding down Control while you zoom in or out with your mouse or trackpad. Once you're zoomed in, your mouse will suddenly start dragging the screen around, which is disconcerting if you are not expecting it. To turn it off, hold down Control and zoom out with your trackpad or mouse wheel. There are a couple of other key sequences that can be invoked accidentally: Option-⌘-8 toggles keyboard zooming on and off, and holding down = or – while pressing Option-⌘ zooms in or out, respectively.

Startup Problems

A misbehaving application is bad enough, but a Mac that won't start properly is truly disconcerting. The good news is that most such problems are repairable. The general method of attack in this case is to get your Mac to a state where you can run Disk Utility and repair the drive. However, there are some situations where you can't even get to that point.

Your Mac beeps at you instead of starting

If your Mac just beeps when you try to start it up, it's trying to tell you something: one beep means there's no memory (RAM) installed, and three beeps means your RAM doesn't pass integrity check. (This goes for Intel Macs only; Power PC Macs have slightly different beeps, but they can't run Lion.) The problem could be a bad RAM module, so you'll need to open up your Mac and replace the module.

Try installing some memory that you're certain is fully functional to see if that resolves the problem. If you don't have any spare memory lying around, try removing each RAM module and replacing them one by one until you've isolated the bad module.

NOTE

If you don't know how to replace memory in your Mac, check the user guide that came with it. Or if your Mac is still under warranty, just take it into an Apple Store for service.

Your hard drive is making noises

If you suspect you've got a physical hard drive problem, you need to check things out quickly before they get much, much worse. If you hear a strange noise coming from your machine, that's an obvious sign of a hard drive problem; but these problems can also be indicated by the computer stalling for

---

several seconds at a time (or making a clicking sound when stalling).

Just as with a car, when a bad sound is emanating from your hard drive, it's usually a bad thing. If you've ever listened to the National Public Radio show *Car Talk*, you know that one of the highlights is when callers try to imitate the sounds their cars are making. If you're inclined to try identifying your hard drive's sound by ear, head over to *http://datacent.com/hard_drive_sounds.php* and take a listen to the sounds of dying drives, sorted by manufacturer.

WARNING

If your hard drive is failing, you're likely to lose more data every moment it's running. If you don't have current backups, your best bet is to replace the drive immediately, and either seek a data recovery professional or, if you don't have the money for that, install the damaged drive in an external drive enclosure and use the GNU ddrescue utility (*http://www.gnu.org/software/ddrescue*) to recover the data on the damaged drive.

If you aren't hearing any obviously unusual sounds but still suspect your hard drive is causing your problems, head to Disk Utility (Applications→Utilities→Disk Utility) and check the S.M.A.R.T. status of the drive.

Using a computer means loving acronyms, and this time the acronym is clever, if a little forced: S.M.A.R.T. stands for Self-Monitoring Analysis and Reporting Technology. The idea behind S.M.A.R.T. is that many hard disk failures are predictable and computer users, if given a heads-up that their hard drive is on the verge of failing, will be able to recover data *before* the failure actually happens. You can discover your drive's S.M.A.R.T. status by opening Disk Utility and selecting the disk you're worried about in the list on the left. In the lower-right part of the Disk Utility window, you'll see the S.M.A.R.T. Status (Figure 4-3): either Verified (everything is fine) or

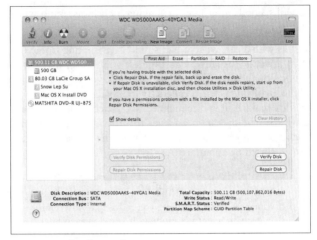

Figure 4-3. This drive is fine

"About to Fail." If you get the "About to Fail" notice, don't waste any time: if your Mac is under warranty, take it into an Apple Store; otherwise, back up your data as soon as possible and start pricing out a new drive.

WARNING

S.M.A.R.T. isn't perfect (that's no surprise—nothing is). You can have a problematic drive that S.M.A.R.T. won't recognize. So if you're having consistent problems and S.M.A.R.T. keeps telling you everything is fine, don't discount the drive as the source of the problems after you've exhausted other fixes.

Startup troubleshooting

Thankfully, the hardware failures just described are relatively rare. Much more common are software failures. Corrupt files, wonky login items, and even font problems can cause a startup failure. These issues are generally repairable, hopefully without

---

data loss. Unfortunately, when you have one of these problems, the cause isn't immediately obvious. When faced with a Mac that won't boot, there are a few things you can try to get your computer back to a usable state:

Restart your Mac

A lot happens when Mac OS X starts up: it checks your Mac's hardware, prepares the system software, and more. During the startup process, there are ample opportunities for something to go wrong, especially right after you install an update to Mac OS X or even an application. If your Mac won't complete the startup sequence, don't panic; simply restart the machine by holding down the power button until you hear a chime; chances are everything will be fine.

WARNING

If you see a flashing question mark when you try to start your Mac, it means that your machine can't find its startup disk. In that case, skip ahead to "Restart in Recovery Mode," below.

Safe Boot

If a simple restart doesn't do the trick, it means you have problems that persist across restarts, so the next step is a Safe Boot. In Safe Mode, all your Mac's startup items are disabled, font caches are cleared, and some other possibly problematic items are avoided. More important, Safe Boot gives you a chance to run Disk Utility, uninstall any software that may be misbehaving, or back up your data before whatever is causing the problem gets worse. To get your Mac to boot into Safe Mode, hold down the Shift key after you hear the startup chime and release the key when you see the spinning wheel appear. Once the Mac is booted, run Disk Utility (Applications→Utilities→Disk Utility).

NOTE

When you're booting in Safe Mode, the Login window automatically appears even if you usually use Automatic Login on your Mac. Don't be alarmed by the change—it's a sign that Safe Mode is working as expected.

Restart in Recovery Mode

Before Lion, one remedy to try when your Mac went bad was to boot from the DVD you either got with your Mac or purchased when you upgraded to Snow Leopard. But since you don't use any physical media—DVD or otherwise—when you install Lion, this trick won't work anymore. Fortunately, Apple realizes that, when problems occur, you might need to boot your Mac from a different source than usual, so Lion includes Recovery Mode.

NOTE

You need to be connected to the Internet to use Recovery Mode to reinstall Lion. The Reinstall Lion option will download every byte of the Lion installer, so you might want to try other fixes before going through with the entire process.

Recovery Mode allows you to boot from a virtual partition called Recovery HD. When you boot into Recovery Mode, you'll find yourself running a special system that lets you restore your Mac from a Time Machine backup, reinstall Lion, use Safari to look for solutions to your problem online, or run Disk Utility. (Don't be afraid to launch Safari even if you're not connected to the Internet; there's a static web page with basic instructions that automatically opens when you launch Safari.)

In addition to Recovery Mode's obvious choices, you can also run Firmware Password Utility, Network Utility, and Terminal by visiting the Utilities drop-down menu at the top of the screen. With all of these options, most users will find the choices presented in the Mac OS X Utilities window sufficient to fix their Mac woes.

Here's how to boot your Mac in Recovery Mode (the process should be familiar if you've booted Macs from alternative disks before): hold down the Option key while starting your Mac. You'll be presented with a screen that shows all the viable startup partitions available. Choose Recovery HD and you'll be well on your way to diagnosing (and hopefully fixing) whatever problem is currently plaguing your Mac.

This section emphasized tools that come with Lion because, well, if you've installed Lion, you have access to these tools. But you should be aware that these tools aren't the only ones available when things go wrong. There are several disk repair programs available (many of which are more powerful than Disk Utility) from third parties, such as DiskWarrior (*http:// www.alsoft.com/DiskWarrior*) and TechTool Pro (*http://www .micromat.com*).

Reset your PRAM

This maneuver gets its own section only because it's one of the oldest troubleshooting techniques in Mac history.

PRAM (parameter random access memory) is where your Mac stores many of its hardware settings. Resetting the PRAM almost never resolves a startup issue, but it's something Apple support usually asks you to do when troubleshooting a problem (and it does, in some rare cases, help). To reset the PRAM, turn on your Mac, *immediately* press and hold Option-⌘-P-R, and continue to hold the keys until your Mac restarts and you hear the startup chime a total of three times. After you do this, you may have to reconfigure some of the system settings (like date, time, and possibly keyboard/mouse settings if you've customized them).

CHAPTER 5

System Preferences

Out of the box, the Mac is a fantastic machine. Its graphical interface is clean and uncluttered, you can use it to accomplish tasks with a minimum of frustration, and everything performs exactly how you expect it to. That honeymoon lasts for somewhere between 10 seconds and a week. While everything is great at first, you'll soon find yourself saying, "Man, it sure would be better if...." When this happens, your first stop should be System Preferences.

Apple knows that different people want different behaviors from their Macs. While Lion can't possibly accommodate everything that everyone might want to do, most of the changes you are likely to want to make are built right into Lion.

System Preferences, which you can get to by clicking the silver-framed gears icon in the Dock (unless you've removed it from the Dock, in which case you can find it in the Applications folder or the menu), is the place to make your Mac uniquely yours. But as you'll see later in this chapter, you can make some tweaks by going beyond System Preferences.

One thing that will inevitably happen while you're adjusting your System Preferences is that you'll make a change and later decide that it was a mistake. For example, say you adjust the time it takes for your Mac to go to sleep and later decide that Apple had it right out of the box. Fortunately, many preference panes feature a Restore Defaults button that resets the settings in that particular pane to the factory defaults.

Lion comes with 28 preference panes, each of which controls a bevy of related preferences. With all those options, how will you remember where to find every setting? For example, are the settings for display sleep under Energy Saver or Displays? Lion makes it easy to find the right preference pane by including a search box in the System Preferences window (Mac OS X is big on search boxes). Type in what you're looking for and the likely choices get highlighted, and you'll see a list of suggested searches (Figure 5-1).

Figure 5-1. Searching for "alerts" in System Preferences. Lion highlights the best candidates and suggests other searches.

Preference Pane Rundown

With so many preference panes, it's hard to keep track of what they all do. This section describes each one.

The System Preferences window is divided into five categories: Personal, Hardware, Internet & Wireless, System, and Other. Other is reserved for non-Apple preference panes and doesn't appear until you've installed at least one third-party preference pane (which usually, but not always, is part of a third-party application).

Some preferences, such as those that affect all users of the computer, need to be unlocked before you can use them. (If a preference pane is locked, there will be a lock icon in its lower left.) These can only be unlocked by a user who has administrative access. On most Macs, the first user you create has those privileges. If you don't have administrative privileges, you'll need to find the person who *does* and have him or her type in the username and password before you can make changes.

General

This preference pane used to be called Appearance. It lets you tweak the look and feel of Mac OS X. The first two options control colors. The Appearance setting controls the overall look of buttons, menus, and windows and has two choices: blue or gray. The Highlight setting controls the color used for text you've selected and offers more choices, including selecting your own color (choose Other).

The second section of this pane lets you decide when you want the scroll bar to show up. "Automatically based on input device" leaves the decision up to your Mac; "When scrolling" means the bars only show up when you're actively scrolling; and, for those who long for the days of Snow Leopard, "Always" keeps them visible all the time. No matter which option you choose you're stuck with gray scroll bars—no more colorful scrolling.

You'll also find options to modify what happens when you click a scroll bar. You can set it to automatically jump to the next page or to the spot that you clicked. The difference between these options is not trivial: if you're looking at a lengthy web page or a thousand-page document, opting for "Jump to next page" means it'll take a lot of clicks to reach the end, whereas "Jump to the spot that's clicked" could shoot all the way to the end in a flash.

You'll also find settings that control smooth scrolling, whether double-clicking a window's title bar minimizes the window, and the size of the icons in Mac OS X's various sidebars. (The most obvious sidebar is in the Finder, but if you adjust the "Sidebar icon size" setting, other sidebars—like Mail's—will also change.)

By default, Lion shows your 10 most recent applications, documents, and servers in the menu's Recent Items submenu, but you can change that number here. And new in Lion, you'll also find a "Restore windows when quitting and re-opening apps" checkbox. This is enabled by default, so if you find yourself annoyed that, say, Safari is reopening all the windows you had open when you restart the app, this is where you can kill that behavior.

Desktop & Screen Saver

The Desktop & Screen Saver preference pane has two tabs. The Desktop tab lets you change the desktop background (also known as wallpaper). You can use the Apple-supplied images, solid colors, or pictures from your iPhoto Library. You can even specify a whole folder of images by clicking the + button in the lower-left corner.

If you pick an image of your own, you can control how the image is displayed by selecting Fill Screen, Fit to Screen, Stretch to Fill Screen, Center, or Tile from the menu to the right of the image preview. If you like a little liveliness, you can tell your computer to change the desktop picture periodically. Apple supplies options ranging from every five seconds to every time you log in or wake from sleep. And if you want your menu bar to be solid instead of see-through, turn off "Translucent menu bar" here.

WARNING

If you choose to change the picture periodically without carefully vetting the source images, you'll likely be presented with something completely useless, confusing, or embarrassing at a random moment.

For something as seemingly mundane as a screensaver, you can get a lot out of the Screen Saver preference pane. Apple includes several built-in screensavers; while most are just abstract animations (sadly no flying toasters), there are two that are a bit more informative: RSS Visualizer lets you watch an RSS feed roll across the screen; to change which feed is displayed, click Options and then change the URL. "Word of the Day" works exactly how you might imagine: you get a word and a definition. But since it's from Apple, it's rendered more beautifully than any other word-of-the-day display you can find.

All your iPhoto pictures are listed here, too; you can choose your entire library or a specific event, album, or MobileMe (soon to be iCloud) gallery. If you specify a collection of pictures, you can change the way the pictures are displayed. The Display Style buttons just below the preview let you choose between Slideshow, Collage, and Mosaic. Click the Options button for even more control over how the pictures are displayed.

Can't decide on a screensaver? Let your Mac select one for you; just check the "Use random screen saver" box. Right below that is another checkbox that superimposes a clock over your screensaver. The Test button lets you see your screensaver in action before you commit to it.

The "Start screen saver" slider beneath the Preview window lets you control how long you have to be inactive before the screensaver kicks in. If you make this delay longer than the delay set for your Mac to sleep, you'll see a yellow warning sign below the slider. Don't worry, nothing bad will happen—you'll just never see the screensaver because, by the time it kicks in, the screen will already be blank.

If you'd like the screensaver to kick in on demand—handy when you're messing around online and the boss walks in—you can set a *hot corner* that lets you invoke the screensaver right away. Click the Hot Corners button in the lower-left corner of the Screen Saver pane and you'll get a new window with options for every corner. Use the drop-down menus to set options for any corner you want; when you move your mouse to that corner, it fires up the screensaver (or does whatever you selected earlier). The only downside of setting hot corners is that you have eight options for each corner, so unless you want to use a modifier key with the corner, you don't have enough corners to use all the options.

NOTE

By using modifier keys (you can choose from Shift, ⌘, Option, and Control), you can get a single corner to do many different things. To add a modifier key to a hot corner, hold down the modifier key while you select what you want the hot corner to do from the Active Screen Corners window's menus. Using modifiers with hot corners not only gives you extra flexibility, it prevents you from accidentally invoking the hot corner action when you're mousing around.

Dock

You won't find a lot of options in the Dock preference pane, but you get control over the most important aspects of the Dock. You can change its size—from illegibly small to ridiculously large—with the aptly named Size slider, which works in real time so you can see the change as you're making it.

If you turn on Magnification, the application or document you're mousing over will become larger than the rest of the items in your Dock. How much larger? Use the Magnification slider to determine that.

If you want to move the Dock somewhere else, click one of the three "Position on screen" radio buttons: Left, Bottom, or Right. (Top isn't an option because you don't want the Dock to compete with the menu bar.)

The "Minimize windows using" menu lets you choose which animation your Mac uses when you minimize a window: the Genie effect or Scale. (These days, this is just a matter of personal preference, but in the early days of Mac OS X, some machines weren't fast enough to render the Genie effect.)

The "Minimize windows into application icon" setting determines where your windows go when you click the yellow button found at the upper left of almost every window. If you leave this unchecked, minimized windows appear on the right side of the Dock (or the bottom of it if you put the Dock on the left or right side of your screen). If you turn on this checkbox, you'll save space in the Dock, but to restore minimized application windows, you'll have to right-click or Control-click the appropriate application's icon in the Dock, select the minimized window from the application's window menu, or invoke Mission Control.

There's also a checkbox labeled "Animate opening applications," which sounds like more fun than it actually is. All it does is control whether applications' icons bounce when you launch them. If you turn this option off, you'll still be able to tell when an application is starting because the dot that appears under it (or next to it, if the Dock is positioned on the left or right) will pulse (unless you've turned off the indicator lights, as explained in a sec). If you turn on "Automatically hide and show the Dock," it will remain hidden until you move the mouse above or next to it.

The blue dots that indicate that an application is running really bother some people. If the blue dots are the bane of your existence, Lion offers something new: a way to turn them off. That's right, unchecking the box next to "Show indicator lights for open applications" will make the blue dots go away. To figure out which apps are running once you've banished the dots, use Mission Control or the Application Switcher.

Mission Control

The Exposé & Spaces preference pane has been replaced by Mission Control (see "Mission Control" on page 6). This pane allows you to adjust how you invoke Mission Control and what happens when you do.

You'll find an option to display Dashboard as a desktop space, which is turned on by default; this setting puts a mini-sized Dashboard screen at the top of your screen with your other spaces. You can opt to have OS X arrange your spaces so that the ones you've used most recently are at the top of the list; if you like to manually set your spaces, uncheck this option. You can also have OS X switch you to a space with an open window when you switch applications. With this option on (which it is by default), if you have a space with a Safari window open, say, and you switch to Safari from another space or full-screen application, the space you switch to will have a Safari window open already. If you turn this option off, you might find yourself in a space without an open window for the application you just switched to, which can be confusing.

You also get to change the shortcuts used to invoke Mission Control, Application windows, Show Desktop, and Show Dashboard. Finally, the Hot Corners button lets you define what your Mac does when you slide your mouse to a corner of the screen (everything from launching Mission Control to putting your display to sleep).

Language & Text

The Language tab of the Language & Text preference pane lets you set the language your Mac uses.

The Text tab is helpful if you spend much time typing. It includes a list of symbol and text substitutions your Mac performs, which lets you do things like type (r) and have it automatically show up as ®. Even better, you can add your *own* substitutions. Click the + button below the list to add whatever text you want substituted and what you want to replace it with; make sure the checkbox to its left is turned on, and your Mac should make that fix automatically from then on. This won't work in every application, but in the supported ones, text substitutions can save you a lot of effort.

On the Text tab, you can also adjust how Mac OS X checks your spelling (the default is automatic by language, but you can have it check everything for French even if your Mac is using English). The Word Break setting affects how words are selected when you double-click on a word, and two drop-down menus let you customize how double and single smart quotes are formatted.

From the Formats tab, you can control the format of the date, time, and numbers on your machine; pick which currency symbols you want to use; and pick between US (imperial) and metric units of measurement.

On the Input Sources tab, you can turn on "Show Input menu in menu bar," which adds a multicolor flag to the otherwise grayscale menu bar. If you check the box labeled Keyboard & Character Viewer (at the top of the list of input sources), you'll be able to launch the Character Viewer and Keyboard Viewer from the menu bar.

The "Input source" list lets you select the language you want to type in. You can choose anything from Afghan Dari to

Welsh, which can mean a lot of scrolling. To speed things up, use the search box at the bottom of the window to find the language you are after.

You can choose as many languages as you like and switch between them using the flag menu extra that appears in your menu bar automatically when you select multiple languages. So you don't have to spend all day changing languages, you can assign the languages globally or locally, respectively, using the radio buttons labeled "Use the same one in all documents" and "Allow a different one for each document."

Security & Privacy

The Security & Privacy preference pane is likely one of the most useful and most overlooked panes in OS X. Take your time setting up these preferences and your data will be much safer than if you stick with the defaults. Ignore this pane and people can see more of your data than you probably want to share, particularly if they have physical access to your Mac. This pane features four tabs: General, FileVault, Firewall, and Privacy.

General tab

If you want to spend 30 seconds making your Mac much safer, the General tab is the place to visit. The first option on this tab is "Require password ___ after sleep or screen saver begins," which lets you fill in that blank with "immediately" or a duration. This makes it so that anyone who wants to use your computer has to enter a password if the screensaver has started or if your Mac has been asleep. This requires more typing on your part, but it is likely worth the inconvenience, especially if you're using your Mac in an open setting. *Not* requiring a password lets anyone who walks by shake your mouse and start poking around. So unless you log out every time you're away from your Mac for more than 30 seconds, seriously consider enabling this option.

The rest of the options in the General tab are for administrators only. You can click the lock in the pane's lower left and then type in an administrator username and password to make changes to the following settings:

Disable automatic login
> Checking this box means all users will have to log in each time the computer is restarted.

Require an administrator password to access system preferences with lock icons
> System Preferences can be powerful, so you wouldn't want just anyone mucking with them. Check this box to force users to authenticate before changing any preferences in a pane that has a lock icon in its lower-left corner.

Log out after __ minutes of activity
> This is a little redundant if you already require a password to wake the computer or get past the screensaver, but for total control, this is a better option. You can force your Mac to log out after any period of inactivity between 1 and 960 minutes (that's 16 hours!). This option will attempt to shut down any applications you're running, so save your work before you wander away (at least until Auto Save is universally supported).

Show a message when the screen is locked
> Turn on this setting and type the message that you want to appear under the login window when your screen is locked.

Automatically update safe downloads list
> This setting, which is turned on by default, lets you opt out of Safari's daily update of safe downloads. These updates help protect you against malware such as MacDefender.mpkg. If you download a dangerous file and it is on Apple's list of known malicious software, you'll get a message telling you to move it to the Trash. (The list is stored on your Mac but gets updated every day.) Turn off this setting and you're taking chances you don't want to take.

Disable remote control infrared receiver

By default, your Mac (unless it's a Mac Pro) will accept input from almost any infrared device. This can pose a security risk and be very annoying if you're using Apple TV and your laptop. Turn this behavior off by checking the box. If you want to use a remote with your Mac but have it ignore all *other* remotes, click the Pair button and follow the instructions that appear.

FileVault tab

Lion includes the new and improved FileVault 2, which provides an extra layer of security for your data. When enabled, FileVault encrypts your entire drive with XTS-AES 128 encryption, the same algorithm used by governments to protect classified data. You might think all that encrypting and decrypting would burden your system, but Mac OS X manages this trick on the fly so you'll never notice a substantial slowdown because of FileVault.

FileVault is turned off by default, but if you decide to enable it, your computer will generate a 24-character recovery key. Committing that key to memory will be a chore, so you can opt to store the key with Apple by choosing the appropriate radio button when the next page pops up. If you do choose to store your key with Apple, it will be encrypted. Apple will only issue the key if you can answer a security question exactly how you answered it during setup. (In other words, you won't have to remember the long security key, but you *will* have to remember the answer.) After you make your choice, restart your Mac and your disk will be encrypted.

WARNING

If you forget your login password *and* lose your recovery key, your data is gone forever.

Firewall tab

The Firewall tab deals with your Internet and network connections. The default setting is off, which means your Mac will listen to and respond to just about anything coming over the network: network traffic, pings, and assorted signals that you're never aware of. Surprisingly, this usually isn't a problem if you use your home network or other trusted network all the time. Your router (or the router of other trusted networks) has a firewall built in, so your Mac's firewall will be a bit redundant. But if you're constantly joining iffy WiFi hotspots with your MacBook, you will likely want to enable the firewall.

To do that, check the lock icon in the pane's lower left and, if it's locked, click it and then type in your administrator name and password. Then simply click the Start button. The light next to the Firewall status entry will turn green to let you know the firewall is up and running.

Now that the firewall is running, you might be wondering what it's actually doing. To find out, click the Advanced button. When you do, you'll get some options that let you tweak how Lion's firewall performs. The first one is "Block all incoming connections"; if you check this box, Lion will only listen to incoming connections for very specific, necessary network communications. You'll also see a message appear warning you that turning on this setting prohibits you from using sharing services such as screen sharing and file sharing.

A less inhibiting option is "Automatically allow signed software to receive incoming connections." With this setting turned on (which it is by default when the firewall is enabled), software that's been signed (meaning its author is known to Apple and Mac OS X has confirmed that it hasn't been altered or corrupted) is allowed to receive incoming connections. Every Apple application on your Mac has been signed, so you won't need to worry about killing any of the built-in applications. You can also give applications the green light even if they aren't signed by clicking the + button; this lets you add them to the list of programs that are allowed to communicate.

If you check the box next to "Enable stealth mode," your Mac will be less visible on the network. For example, should some nefarious person try to scan all ports at your IP for a way in, they'll get no response; it'll seem like no computer exists at the scanned IP address. However, network activity you engage in, such as visiting a web page or checking your email, can reveal your presence on the network.

Privacy

This tab is new in Lion. It includes an option that allows your computer to send certain data to Apple; this is turned on by default. There's also an area where you can turn off location services (also on by default) for applications that try to determine where you are.

Spotlight

The Spotlight preference pane has two tabs. The Search Results tab lets you adjust the order of results returned by Spotlight searches (drag items in the list here to change their order in results) and change the Spotlight menu and window shortcuts. The Privacy tab allows you to exclude folders and disks (but not individual files) from Spotlight's searches. For more on Spotlight, see "Searching with Spotlight" on page 91.

Universal Access

Universal Access settings are designed for people with impairments that prevent them from using their Macs in a standard manner—but they can be fun for *anyone* who wants to use a Mac in a nonstandard manner.

At the bottom of the pane are two checkboxes: one that lets you enable access for assistive devices (such as touchscreens and pointing devices) and one that adds a Universal Access menu extra to the menu bar.

Each of the preference pane's four tabs controls a different method of interacting with your Mac.

Seeing tab

This tab includes radio buttons for turning VoiceOver (Mac OS X's built-in screen-reading utility) on or off. You'll also find buttons for enabling screen zooming. If you want to customize how your Mac zooms, click the Options button to access a bunch of zoom-related settings. The Display section of the Seeing tab has two radio buttons: "Black on white" is the standard display; "White on black" inverts your screen so that everything from your desktop image to your Dock icons is displayed in the opposite colors—black turns white, green turns purple, etc. If you want to eschew color altogether, check the "Use grayscale" box (a great way to simulate a retro computing experience). The Enhance Contrast slider bumps up the contrast, making subtle details harder to see but text easier to read.

The "Zoom in window" setting allows you to magnify a single window instead of your entire screen. Clicking the Options button next to it lets you fine-tune the zoomed window: set the magnification, invoke a preview rectangle, smooth out images, and decide whether you want to zoom to follow your keyboard. You'll also discover radio buttons that control how the screen behaves when zoomed. You can have the screen move to wherever the pointer is, move only when the pointer reaches an edge, or move so that the pointer is at (or near) the center of the image. You'll also get an option to use a scroll wheel and a modifier key of your choice to zoom the window.

Hearing tab

On the Hearing tab, you can choose to have your Mac's screen flash instead of using audio alerts (quite useful when your Mac is muted), and there's an option to play stereo audio as mono.

Keyboard tab

For some, pressing the various keystrokes required to operate a Mac can be challenging. Sticky Keys, which is controlled by the options at the top of the Keyboard tab, solves this problem. Instead of being forced to hit multiple keys at the same time (such as ⌘ and P to print), enabling Sticky Keys makes your Mac interpret pressing ⌘ and then pressing P as if you'd pressed them simultaneously. You'll also find checkboxes that allow you to turn Sticky Keys on or off by tapping the Shift key five times, enable beeping when a modifier key is pressed, and display the pressed keys on screen as you press them (these last two settings only work if Sticky Keys is turned on).

Another option is Slow Keys, which puts a delay between when you press a key and when your Mac accepts it. Turn this feature on and there will be a delay between the time you press a key and the time when OS X recognizes that you did so (you can adjust that period with the Acceptance Delay slider). If your fingers move slowly, this can save a lot of unwanted repeated keystrokes. The "Use click key sounds" checkbox tells your Mac to make one sound when a key is depressed and a different sound when the key is accepted.

Mouse tab (Mouse & Trackpad tab on MacBooks)

Those who have trouble using a mouse or trackpad can control the mouse cursor with the keyboard instead by heading to this tab and turning on Mouse Keys. This is also where you set the length of time you have to hold the directional keys before the cursor starts to move. You can also specify the cursor's maximum speed and, if you have trouble seeing the cursor, its size. If you use this feature, you'll be happy to see that, in Lion, the cursor looks much better when magnified than in previous versions of OS X. Click the Trackpad Options or Mouse Options button to fine-tune things even more.

CDs and DVDs

If you have an optical disk drive in your Mac, this preference pane controls what your Mac does when you insert an optical disk. You can even tell it to do different things depending on the type of disk: a blank CD or DVD, a music CD, a picture CD, or a video DVD. When you click one of the drop-down menus, you'll see Apple's recommended action (the audio CD menu includes Open iTunes, for example), but you aren't limited to just the predefined options. Choosing "Open other application..." will bring up your Applications folder so you can choose any program you like. Or you can opt to have a script run when you insert a disk; when you choose this option, you'll be presented with the familiar window that lets you browse to the repository where the script you want to use is saved.

Displays

If you own a laptop or an iMac, you probably won't visit this preference pane until you need to connect a second monitor or projector. On the other hand, if you're a color perfectionist or need to connect your Mac to a non-Apple display, stopping by the Displays pane is necessary. This is where you can control your monitor's resolution, color depth, brightness, and color to fit your needs.

If you're using multiple displays, you can set the location of the menu bar, enable display mirroring, and also configure the spatial arrangement of each screen so they correspond to how the displays are physically arranged.

This is also where you'd *expect* to find an option to run two or more applications in Full Screen mode. Sadly, that's not an option. You can have 10 screens, but when you use a full-screen app, the other screens will change to a gray linen pattern conveying no useful information.

Energy Saver

You get different options in this preference pane depending on what kind of Mac you're using. On a MacBook, you'll see two tabs—Battery and Power Adapter—which makes sense because you'll likely want different settings when you're using the power adapter than when you're relying on the battery. Also, the "Show battery status in the menu bar" checkbox is turned on by default, giving you a quick way to see how much power you have left. (If you feel that the menu bar on your Mac is simply too crowded, unchecking this box will free up a tiny bit of space.)

The options on both laptops and desktops are very similar. The slider next to "Computer sleep" allows you to define the delay between the time you stop using your Mac and the time it enters sleep mode, a low-power mode that uses much less power than when it's "awake." Although Lion will restart all your apps when you restart, waking from sleep is a much faster process. (The two tabs on a laptop—Battery and Power Adapter—allow you to set different values for when your Mac sleeps depending on its current power source.) The "Display sleep" slider adjusts how long it takes for your screen to turn off to save power (again, you can set two different values if you're on a laptop).

Under the sliders are some checkboxes (they vary slightly between the Battery and Power Adapter tabs):

Put the hard disk(s) to sleep when possible
> This checkbox will put your drives to sleep when OS X thinks it's a good idea. (Some hard drives have this functionality built in, but Mac OS X will put the drives to sleep before their firmware would normally do so.)

Wake for network access
> If you use Back to My Mac or have a copy of Apple Remote Desktop, you'll probably want to check this box, which allows your Mac to wake up when you want to log in remotely.

Automatically reduce brightness before display goes to sleep

Checking this box means that your display will noticeably dim before it becomes completely black. Any mouse or keyboard action will bring the display back to full brightness.

Slightly dim the display when using this power source (laptops only)

This option is on the Battery tab. As you can probably guess, this is supposed to extend battery life by making the display use less energy when you're relying on battery power. In practice, most people don't notice the difference in battery life.

Start up automatically after a power failure

Checking this box means that if the power flickers, your Mac will start up again as soon as the power comes back on. Your Mac doesn't really know that the power has gone; it just knows that shutdown protocol wasn't followed. If you accidentally hit the off button on a surge protector, your Mac will start up when the button is moved back to the on position, too. (For obvious reasons, this option isn't available on MacBooks' Battery tab.)

Restart automatically if the computer freezes

This has been an option in previous server versions of OS X, but with Lion it's on every install of OS X. Checking this box tells your Mac to monitor your computer for kernel panics and system freezes. If you're worried that checking this box could result in spontaneous reboots, don't worry too much. The system uses a timer and response system, so your Mac will need to be frozen for at least five minutes before it restarts.

If you're a very consistent person, you can get the best of all worlds by clicking the Schedule button. This brings up a pane where you can tell your Mac when you want it to start up or wake and when you want it to shut down, sleep, or restart by choosing the schedule from the pop-up menus and entering times in the boxes.

Sounds fantastic, right? Well, maybe the Schedule feature isn't all that it could be. You have to be logged in and your computer has to be awake for it to shut down at a specific time. So this is a great option if you're sitting in front of your Mac when you want it to shut down, but unless you're comfortable leaving your Mac unattended and awake while you're logged in, the automatic shutdown option isn't of much use.

Happily, you don't have to worry about these problems if you want your Mac to wake or start automatically; automatic startup works exactly as you'd expect. For example, if you're sitting in front of your Mac every weekday by 8:07, having your Mac automatically start up at 8:03 can save you a few minutes of waiting each day.

Keyboard

The Keyboard preference pane is where you can change key commands (see Chapter 8 for a list of common ones) and how your keyboard responds to typing. The pane is divided into two tabs—Keyboard and Keyboard Shortcuts—and includes a Set Up Bluetooth Keyboard button. If you've got a Bluetooth keyboard that your computer hasn't recognized automatically, click this button to make Mac OS X attempt to pair with it.

Keyboard tab

This tab has two sliders: the Key Repeat slider allows you to adjust how frequently a key will register if you hold it down, and the Delay Until Repeat slider controls how long you have to hold a key down before your Mac starts registering that key repeatedly. The Keyboard tab also gives you the option to use all the numbered F keys as standard function keys. If you turn on this option, those keys won't work the same way; for example, pressing F10 won't mute your Mac, it will invoke Exposé (to mute your Mac, you'll need to press the Fn *and* F10 at the same time). Turning on the "Show Keyboard & Character Viewers in menu bar" checkbox creates a menu extra that gives you easy access to characters (arrows and such) with the

Character Viewer and the Keyboard Viewer's simulated keyboard that shows what the modifier keys do when pressed.

Click Input Sources to see the "Input source" list, which lets you type in different languages. Select the language you want to type in, anything from Afghan Dari to Welsh. That can mean a lot of scrolling, so to speed things up, you can use the search box at the bottom of the window to find the language you're after.

You can choose as many languages as you like and switch between them at will using the flag menu extra that appears in your menu bar automatically when you select multiple languages. So that you don't have to spend all day changing languages, you can choose to assign the languages globally or locally using the radio buttons labeled "Use the same one in all documents" and "Allow a different one for each document," respectively.

Keyboard Shortcuts tab

This is where you can adjust the key commands used by your Mac. The left side of the pane has a list of applications and features so you can more easily locate the ones you want to change. To actually change a key command, double-click it in the list on the right and then press the key you want to use instead. You can use the function keys or keys with modifiers as your new choice. Figure 5-2 shows an example.

To add a new key command, click the + button. You'll see a pop-up menu of applications that you can add keyboard commands to. Select an application, type the *exact* name of the menu command you want to create a keyboard shortcut for into the Menu Title box, and then type the key you want to use as the shortcut. For example, there's no keyboard command for customizing the toolbar in the Finder. To create one, select Finder from the pop-up menu, type `Customize Toolbar...` (*with* the dots) into the Menu Title box, and then click the Keyboard Shortcut field and type your shortcut. Now when a Finder window is active, you can hit that key and the

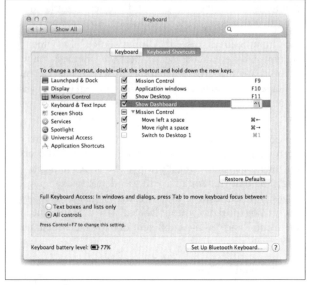

Figure 5-2. Changing the key command for Dashboard

Customize Toolbar window will show up. As a bonus, the key command you added will also appear next to the command's name in the Finder's View menu. If you tire of your custom key command, click the shortcut once and then hit the – key; your key command will be banished from the preference pane *and* from the Finder. The Restore Defaults button (on the right side under the list of keyboard shortcuts) will also kill your custom key command and any other changes you've made.

Below the two lists, this tab also includes a setting for Full Keyboard Access (a way for you to interact with your Mac without using the mouse). If you switch this setting from the default "Text boxes and lists only" to "All controls," you'll be able to use Tab to move from field to field in most applications.

Mouse

Plan on using a mouse with your Mac? This preference pane lets you set up a Bluetooth mouse and customize your mousing options.

NOTE

One of the most off-putting changes for a lot of people when they first use Lion is the OS's new scrolling behavior: When you scroll with two fingers or with a mouse wheel, moving your fingers or the wheel *up* (away from you) makes the current page or document scroll *down*, and vice versa. It's called "Scroll with finger direction" and it works perfectly on the iPhone and other iOS devices. When you put this same behavior on Macs, it still works fine—except that it's exactly the *opposite* of how scrolling has worked since the first Mac rolled out.

You'll quickly get used to new scrolling, but if you just can't stand it or you use multiple OSes and want some consistency, head to the Mouse and Trackpad preference panes and turn off "Scroll with finger direction."

Magic Mouse options

If you've got a Magic Mouse, the Point & Click tab of this preference pane allows you to turn "Scroll with finger direction" on or off, decide whether you want a secondary click (known as a "right-click" to everyone but Apple) with your Magic Mouse and how you want said click enacted, and turn smart zooming off or on. You also get a mouse battery–level indicator and a slider for adjusting tracking (how fast the mouse pointer moves on screen in response to physical mouse movements).

On the More Gestures tab, you can turn on "Swipe between pages," "Swipe between full-screen apps," and an option to launch Mission Control with a double tap. Each gesture comes with a nifty movie explaining how to pull off the necessary taps and swipes. To watch the movie, put your cursor over the gesture you're interested in and the instructional video will play automatically.

Mighty Mouse options

If you're using a Mighty Mouse, you'll find sliders for adjusting tracking, double-click, and scrolling speeds. You'll also see pop-up menus for every part of the Mighty Mouse that can detect pushes. Each menu lets you specify what happens when you press that button. You can choose from a multitude of actions to assign to each button, including secondary clicks and application launching.

After you're done setting up the buttons, you can control how the Mighty Mouse scrolls by choosing from the pop-up menu next to Scrolling. You can turn it off, have it scroll vertically only, scroll vertically and horizontally, or scroll 360 degrees.

You can also set up your Mighty Mouse to zoom by checking the box next to Zoom. You get to select the modifier key that will invoke zooming when you're using the scroll ball. If you click the Options button, you'll find some settings that let you fine-tune its scrolling behavior.

If you're using a non-Apple mouse

Some people don't like Apple's mice, and that's OK—your Mac will happily work with non-Apple mice. Some mice ship with custom drivers, but most can work with your Mac straight out of the box. The customization options you see in the Mouse preference pane depend on the model you're using.

Trackpad

Your options here depend on which MacBook you use. On newer MacBooks with multitouch trackpads (which were introduced on the MacBook Air in 2008), you'll get the options described in the multitouch section below. (You'll get that same set of options if you're using Apple's Magic Trackpad.) If you have an older MacBook, you'll get a different set of options, though some of the settings are the same as on multitouch machines.

Multitouch trackpads

In the Trackpad preference pane, you'll be able to adjust your MacBook's tracking speed, set up a Bluetooth trackpad, and configure gestures. On the "Point and Click" tab, you can enable "Tap to click" (which makes your Mac interpret a light tap as a click), "Secondary click" (a.k.a. "right-clicking"), "Look up" (a feature that looks up words with Mac OS X's built-in Dictionary), and three-finger dragging.

When you click the Scroll & Zoom tab, you'll find the following options: "Scroll with finger direction," "Zoom in or out by pinching," "Use two fingers to Smart zoom," and "Rotate images using two fingers."

The More Gestures tab includes six different options to customize. You'll be able to turn on "Swipe between pages" and tell your Mac how you want to gesture to invoke that function. You can do the same with "Swipe between full-screen apps," Mission Control, and App Exposé. Launchpad and "Show Desktop gestures" aren't customizable; you can only turn them on or off.

As with the Magic Mouse, these gestures aren't always self-explanatory, so each gesture comes with a little movie showing you how to pull it off. Hover over the option you want explained and the associated movie will automatically start playing. (One supposes it has been a good time for hand models in the Cupertino area.)

Print & Scan

This preference pane, unsurprisingly, is where you add and remove printers and scanners. To add a device, click the tiny + button on the left side of the pane. Lion will automatically look for nearby printers and scanners and set them up for you. To remove a printer or scanner, select it in the list and then click the – button beneath the list. The rest of the options you see in this pane depend on the exact model of printer or scanner you have installed.

Sound

The Sound preference pane is divided into three tabs: Sound Effects, Output, and Input. The "Output volume" setting is always visible at the bottom of the pane, regardless of which tab you're using. There's a checkbox below that volume slider that lets you get rid of the Volume menu extra. If you're wondering how you'll control the volume with the menu extra gone, remember that you can use the keyboard for that trick; use the F10–F12 keys on Apple keyboards.

Sound Effects tab

The Sound Effects tab allows you to choose an alert sound. To preview a sound, click it in the list or use the arrows to move up and down. Lion gives you plenty of options for audio alerts, so hopefully you can find something to your liking.

The next question is where do you want the alert sounds to come from? If you have speakers plugged into your Mac, you can opt to send the sound through those speakers or through the computer's built-in speaker(s).

Below that is a slider for adjusting the alert volume if, for example, you want your alert sounds to be softer than the rest of the sounds coming out of your Mac (you don't want Basso walking all over iTunes, right?). Note that the maximum alert volume is the same as the master volume for your system, so if you want alerts to be the loudest noise coming out of your Mac, you're out of luck unless you can turn down the volume of other sound-generating programs.

Finally, you get two or three checkboxes so you hear the sounds you want and skip the sounds you don't. By checking the box next to each entry, you can:

- Play or silence user interface sounds (such as the noise the Trash makes when being emptied).
- Play feedback when volume is changed (with this turned on, if you hit a volume key or move the volume slider, the alert sound will play at the new volume).

Output tab

The Sound Effects tab lets you decide which speakers play alert sounds. On the Output tab, you get to decide where everything *else* is played. For example, you can choose between your Mac Pro's internal speaker (not great for an immersive media experience) or the top-of-the-line speakers you plugged into the optical out port. Headphones are a special case, as plugging headphones in mutes the internal speakers.

You also might get some extra options depending on your hardware. For example, if you're using the built-in speakers on an iMac or MacBook, you get to adjust the left-right balance with a slider.

Input tab

This tab is where you control your Mac's "ears." If you're using anything other than a Mac Mini or Mac Pro, your computer has a built-in internal microphone, which is the default selection for sound input. This means that any audio chats, video chats, or podcasts you record will get recorded via that internal mic. If you want to use a USB microphone instead, plug it in and select it from the list on this tab.

Another option on this tab is "Input volume," which controls how "hot" (as they say in the radio business) the sound coming into your Mac will be. Turn it all the way up and anyone you're chatting with will reach for his or her volume controls a millisecond into the conversation.

Turning on "Use ambient noise reduction" tells your Mac to ignore the sounds going on around you—screaming kids, howling wolves, what have you. It isn't perfect, but it helps when you're chatting or, more importantly, using voice commands with your Mac.

Mail, Contacts & Calendars

This preference pane is new in Lion. Instead of setting up mail accounts in Mail, juggling calendars in iCal, and so on, this pane lets you set up your accounts once in a centralized location. iChat, Mail, Address Book, and other apps use the information you enter here to keep you current.

When you first open this pane, it will look on your Mac for email and chat accounts and automatically add them. If you're setting up a new Mac, this pane comes with iCloud (when it's released), Microsoft Exchange, MobileMe, Gmail, Yahoo!, and AOL accounts preconfigured, so if you're using one of those (and you probably are), just click the Add Account button and select the service you use. As you add the service, a window will pop up allowing you to check the services you want to use (chat, calendars, and mail) from that provider.

If your service isn't listed, click Other and get ready to do a little bit of work. The prelisted services all provide calendars, chat, contact, and mail accounts; to get the same functions from another service, you'll have to set these up individually. Figure 5-3 gives you an idea of what you're in for.

MobileMe

As of this writing, MobileMe is still around, but when iOS 5 is released, MobileMe will disappear and be replaced by iCloud. If you have a MobileMe account, taking the time to set it up will likely ease the transition to iCloud.

With MobileMe, you can sync your data to the MobileMe service (and, in turn, to other Macs, iPhones, iPod Touches,

Figure 5-3. You can avoid the hassle of creating an account here by getting a free Gmail or Yahoo! account

and iPads). MobileMe also includes iDisk, which lets you store lots of data on Apple's servers. For more on MobileMe—and iCloud, once it's released—head to this book's website (*http://oreilly.com/catalog/9781449310585*).

Network

You can guess what this preference pane does: it controls your network configuration. At the top of the pane is the Location menu. By default, it's set to Automatic, but if you use your Mac in more than one place, you might want to add a location. To do so, pick Edit Locations from this menu; in the window that appears, click the + sign and then add your location. ("Location" is OS X networking-speak for a group of saved configurations for network ports. Chances are you won't need to manage these manually.)

On the left side of the Network pane, you'll see all the ways your Mac can connect to the network (typically WiFi, Ethernet, and FireWire, but this can vary according to the model of your Mac). If a network is connected, it'll have a green light next to it (unconnected networks have red lights). It's possible to have more than one active network connection—a WiFi connection and an Ethernet connection, perhaps. If that's the case, you can drag the connections around in the list to match your preferred order of connecting. For example, dragging Ethernet to the top will force your Mac to use the Ethernet connection before the WiFi connection.

To the right of the list of networks, you'll find information about and options for your current network. This is where you can find your IP address and settings related to the kind of connection you're using (like a Turn Wi-Fi Off button, for example). For wired networks, you'll get to pick how you want to configure IPv4. You can get this information from your ISP, but most use DCHP and your Mac will be able to take care of this for you. You'll also see an Advanced button that you can click to bring up six different tabs. Configuring these tabs usually isn't necessary and is beyond the scope of this pocket guide.

The best thing about the Network preference pane is the "Assist me" button at the bottom of it. If you're having problems setting up your network, clicking this button and following the directions will likely solve your problems. The Revert button, as you can guess, will undo any changes you've made to your network settings, and Apply tells the preference pane to implement your changes.

Bluetooth

Predictably, this is the go-to panel if you're using a Bluetooth device or if you want to display a Bluetooth status icon in your menu bar. This panel includes a list of all the discoverable Bluetooth devices nearby (in other words, ones your Mac can connect to) and their current connection statuses. If you click the Sharing Setup button, you'll open the Sharing preference pane (described next). If you click the Advanced button, you'll get the following options:

- Open Bluetooth Setup Assistant at startup if no keyboard is detected
- Open Bluetooth Setup Assistant at startup if no mouse or trackpad is detected
- Allow Bluetooth devices to wake this computer
- Reject incoming audio requests

The descriptions below each item explain what they're for. You'll also find an area that lists (and allows you to adjust) Bluetooth devices that use serial ports on your Mac.

Sharing

The Sharing preference pane allows you to share a variety of files and bits of hardware over your network (all of these options are off by default):

DVD or CD Sharing
> This option allows other computers to use the optical drive in your Mac. There's also a checkbox to have your Mac ask you before anyone accesses your computer's optical drive.

Screen Sharing
> Allows other computers to view your screen and control your computer over the network. You can specify which users are allowed to connect or allow all users. If you'd like to let people connect from non-Mac computers, click Computer Settings and then enable the VNC (Virtual Network Computing) option; they'll need a VNC client such as RealVNC or TightVNC for this to work.

File Sharing
> File sharing allows others to access your shared files over the network, a nifty way to trade files. If you turn this option on, make sure you create a strong password.

If you turn on file sharing, users on other computers have a few ways to connect. If the computers you want to share files with are on the same local network, they can get to your computer by heading to the Finder's menu bar and choosing Go→Connect to Server. The address they'll need to access your computer is your Mac's name with .*local* appended.

It may be even easier, though. Mac OS X features a zero-configuration networking protocol called Bonjour. You'll see other computers that you can access in the sidebar of a Finder window.

Users will have to supply a username and password to connect. You may want to set up a sharing-only user (see "Setting up accounts" on page 38) for this.

If you want to access your files from another Mac while away from your home or work network, you can use Back to My Mac, which was part of MobileMe and will be part of iCloud. For specific instructions on using the iCloud version, head to this book's web page (*http://oreilly.com/catalog/0636920021599*).

Printer Sharing

Checking this box turns your Mac into a print server. If you're on a laptop and want to print something in the basement, you won't have to haul your carcass over to the printer or even send the file to the Mac connected to the printer for later printing. Just check the Printer Sharing box on the Mac that's hooked up to the printer and you can print from anywhere on your local area network.

Scanner Sharing

This is Printer Sharing's less-used little brother, and it works in much the same way: if you've got a scanner connected to the host Mac, you can use it from a remote computer. This feature is new in Lion.

Web Sharing

> This *isn't* the box to check if you want to share your Internet connection; instead, this box lets you share web pages in your Sites folder. Turning on Web Sharing reveals a URL for your computer's websites and your personal website (which happens to be the computer's website with *~username* appended) that people on your local network can visit. The URLs will be something like *http://yourcomputername/* and *http://yourcomputername/~yourhomefoldername*.

> Your website will be available over Bonjour networking as well; you can configure Safari to display Bonjour sites in its bookmarks by opening Safari's Preferences, going to the Bookmarks pane, and turning on all the Include Bonjour checkboxes.

Remote Login

> This lets users connect to your Mac over SSH (Secure Shell). To do that, you'll need to open a Terminal window (Applications→Utilities→Terminal) and either use the *ssh* command-line utility or select Shell→New Remote Connection.

Remote Management

> If you have a copy of Apple Remote Desktop and want to use it to connect to your Mac, make sure this box is checked. If you're curious, Remote Management is a lot like screen sharing, except that it's designed for people controlling more than one Mac at a time, as you might find in a classroom setting.

Remote Apple Events

> Checking this box will let other Macs send Apple Events to your computer. What are Apple Events? They are wide ranging, but just about anything AppleScript can do can be an Apple Event.

Xgrid Sharing

> Xgrid allows intensive computing tasks to be broken up and worked on by individual Macs. This option is mainly

used for scientific research and other processor-intensive tasks.

Internet Sharing

This setting lets you share your Internet connection with other computers. You can choose to share a wired connection via AirPort or share an AirPort connection with another computer wired to yours. If you're sharing a wired connection via AirPort, you can choose to add some security measures.

Bluetooth Sharing

Checking this box allows Bluetooth devices to interact with your Mac. The options here let you customize your Mac's behavior when receiving files, designate a folder for the files your Mac accepts over Bluetooth, set browsing behavior, and designate which folders users can browse on your Mac.

Users & Groups

Using this preference pane, an administrator can manage accounts. To add or delete accounts, use the + and – buttons under the list of users. (For a complete discussion of managing accounts, see "User Accounts" on page 35.)

Clicking Login Options at the bottom of the list of users lets you enable or disable automatic login. You'll also get to choose what appears in the login window: the "Name and password" setting is more secure than "List of users" because it means that anyone trying to get into your Mac will need to guess both your username *and* password. You also get to decide whether to show the Restart, Sleep, and Shut Down buttons on the login window; show the Input menu in the login window; show password hints; and use VoiceOver in the login window.

Finally, you can enable fast user switching, which—as its name implies—lets you switch between accounts without logging out first. You'll still need a password to get back to your account, but if an application was running when you switched users, it'll be running when you come back to your account.

The drop-down menu next to this setting lets you view users by full name, short name, or icon. For more on fast user switching, see "Logging In" on page 44.

Fast user switching is nifty, but you might be wondering if you aren't better off using the Resume feature of Lion, which restarts everything automatically when you log back in. While the end result is the same, fast user switching is actually a little faster than relying on Resume because the applications aren't fully shut down when you use fast user switching.

Parental Controls

Parental Controls are Mac OS X's way of protecting your kids while they are on the Internet. This preference pane takes some of the worry out of allowing a child to use the Internet unsupervised by letting you set up a variety of rules and filters. These control not only where your child can go on the Internet but also what programs they can use and even who they can chat and email with. The pane has five tabs.

NOTE

While Parental Controls are designed for parents whose kids use their computers, you can use them to manage any user who isn't an administrator.

Apps tab

This tab allows you to enable a simplified Finder and control which applications the user can run. If you're enabling content controls, controlling which applications the managed user can run is essential.

To give particular applications the green light, click the box next to Limit Applications and then use the settings underneath it to choose applications. Turn off the "Allow User to Modify the Dock" checkbox to revoke that privilege. Clicking the Logs button reveals where your kid has been going, shows where she's tried to go, and gives you access to her iChat transcripts. See something you don't like? Hit the Block button at the bottom of the window to add the website or chat participant to the list of blocked sites or individuals.

Web tab

This tab is concerned with where people can go while they're on the Internet. It offers three levels of control:

Allow unrestricted access to websites
> Clicking this radio button allows complete access to the Web.

Try to limit access to adult websites automatically
> If you click this button, Mac OS X will rely on filters and lists of adult websites and try to block them. It's surprisingly accurate. The downside is that the filters also block all https (secure) websites, so if your teen is doing online banking, she won't be able to access her account. If you want to allow a site or specifically exclude a site that isn't caught by the filter, click the Customize button.

Allow access to only these websites
> This is the most restrictive option. The sites a managed user can visit are limited to the ones listed here, which have been preapproved by Apple. To add or delete sites, use the + and – buttons below the list.

People tab

This tab limits who the managed user can interact with via Mail, iChat, or both. Once you've checked the appropriate box(es), you have to approve any person who wants to email or chat with your kids by clicking the + button and then typing in the person's email address and instant messaging information.

Time Limits tab

This tab allows you to set a maximum amount of time the computer can be used per day and when. Just drag the sliders to set the durations for weekdays and weekends. Use the Bedtime section to restrict when the user can be on the computer.

Other tab

This tab includes four options: hiding profanity in OS X's built-in dictionaries, preventing the user from printing documents, preventing the user from burning CDs and DVDs, and preventing the user from changing the password to his or her account.

Date & Time

The Date & Time tab of this preference pane is where you can set the date using the calendar interface (or just by typing it in) and set the time. The "Set date and time automatically" checkbox (which is turned on by default) tells your Mac to fetch the current date and time from the server that's selected in the menu to the right. You can modify your date and time formats by clicking the Open Language & Text button; see "Language & Text" on page 123 for details.

The Time Zone tab controls the time zone your Mac uses. There's a checkbox that tells your Mac to do this automatically, but if it guesses wrong, you can set it manually by clicking on the map or providing the name of a major city in your time zone.

The Clock tab gives you the option of showing the current date and time in the menu bar, allows you to choose how the time is displayed there, and lets you tweak a few other options. You can also have your Mac announce the time every hour, half hour, or 15 minutes. Click the Customize Voice button and you'll be able to change the voice used to announce the time, how loud it is, and even how quickly it speaks.

Software Update

This preference is focused on getting updates for Mac OS X and telling you which updates you've already installed. (Note that Software Update only updates Apple software.) The Scheduled Check tab allows you to schedule when your computer checks with Apple's servers for new updates. Uncheck the "Check for updates" box and you'll have to check for them manually. You also have the option to automatically download updates. This can be useful because, as soon as an important update is downloaded (automatically, behind the scenes), you'll be notified and can install it without having to wait for the download to complete. The Installed Software tab contains a list of all the updates you've installed.

Speech

If you've ever seen *Star Trek*, you've probably dreamed of talking to your computer and having it do your bidding. Mac OS X can do that. Getting the most out of the Speech feature requires some tweaking, though. The Speech preference pane has two tabs: Speech Recognition (the exciting "control your Mac with your voice" stuff) and the more mundane "Text to Speech" tab, which gives you control over how your Mac reads text.

Speech Recognition tab

This tab is where you turn Speakable Items (short verbal commands you give to your computer like "What time is it?") on or off. This tab has two subtabs: Settings and Commands.

On the Settings tab, the Microphone menu allows you to choose which mic to use. You can choose one that's plugged into your Mac or go with the built-in mic (assuming your Mac has one). The Calibrate button opens a window where you can practice giving your Mac verbal commands. The Change Key button lets you pick which key you press to tell Mac OS X to start listening.

The Listening Method section allows you to have the Mac listen either only while you're pressing the Listening Key or after you speak a keyword. If you decide to go with a keyword, you can choose whether the keyword is optional and whether it's is required before or after the command. The default keyword is "computer," but it is probably wiser to go with a word that you don't say when frustrated (as in "stupid computer"). "Rosebud" works well; just don't watch *Citizen Kane* while computing. There's also an Upon Recognition option to make your Mac to play a sound to acknowledge that it has received your command (you get to choose the sound).

The Commands tab is where you control exactly what speakables are allowed. In the "Select a command set" list, turn a particular set of commands on or off by checking the box next to that set (highlighting an item in the list displays a short explanation of what commands are included in that set). For example, you could choose Address Book and then click Configure to see a list of all your contacts. Using speakable commands, you could tell your Mac to open an email to one of your contacts. Uncheck a particular contact and you won't be able to use speech commands to reach that person.

Click the Open Speakable Items Folder button to display, well, the Speakable Items folder (Figure 5-4). This is where all your speakable actions are stored. You have a bevy of choices built right in, and you can always create your own using Automator.

NOTE

If you're going to make your own speakable items, you have to save them in this folder. No big deal, right? In Snow Leopard and earlier versions of OS X, that was true. But in Lion, the Speakable Items folder is inside the user's Library folder, which is invisible. Because of that, the easiest way to get at this folder to move your own speakables into it is to use the Open Speakable Items Folder button in the Speech preference pane.

Figure 5-4. A small sampling of speakable items for Mail

Text to Speech tab

This tab gives you control over how Mac OS X reads text. It also lets you decide whether you want to hear an announcement when an alert is displayed or when an application needs your attention. To select which voice your Mac uses, select your favorite from the System Voice menu (click Play to preview each one). The Speaking Rate slider controls how quickly the voice speaks. If you want to have your Mac read text you've selected, turn on "Speak selected text when the key is pressed" and, if you like, click Change Key to pick your own key combination for this feature.

Time Machine

Time Machine is Apple's solution to the annoyance of making backups. In this preference pane, you can choose where, what, and when to back up. For more information, see "Time Machine" on page 176.

Startup Disk

The Startup Disk pane allows you to specify which currently attached disk you wish to use to start your Mac. You can use any valid startup disk (your choices will show up in the pane), including DVDs and external disks. Clicking Restart reboots your system using the selected disk. You can also choose your startup disk while your Mac is starting by pressing and holding the Option key.

If your Mac has a FireWire port, you can also choose to start the machine in Target Disk Mode. This turns your high-priced Mac into a glorified hard drive, but it is extremely useful for transferring data and preferences and repairing troublesome hard disks.

Non-Apple Preference Panes

After you install a non-Apple application that has a preference pane of its own, you'll see that pane in a new section of System Preferences labeled Others (as shown in Figure 5-5). These panes work the same as Apple's own, and they allow you to control aspects of the program or feature you added. For example, if you install Perian (*http://www.perian.org*) so your Mac can display a greater variety of video types, the way to interact with Perian is through its preference pane.

One of the most common questions about third-party preference panes isn't how to *use* them; it's how to get rid of them. If the third-party application doesn't include an option to uninstall its preference pane, you can manually uninstall the pane by right-clicking or Control-clicking it and selecting Remove (see Figure 5-5).

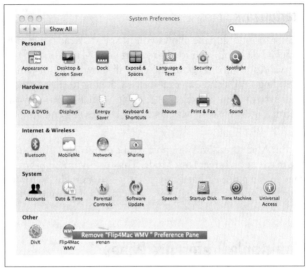

Figure 5-5. Removing a third-party preference pane

CHAPTER 6

Built-in Applications and Utilities

When you install Lion, a number of applications and utilities come along for the ride. You'll get the predictable apps like Safari, and the boring-yet-useful utilities like Activity Monitor, as well as brand-new applications like Launchpad. And some of the older applications, such as Mail, have been radically upgraded.

Applications Installed with Lion

This section gives you a quick rundown of all the applications installed by default with Lion. Note that the list only covers applications that come with a Lion install—if you have a brand-new Mac or are upgrading an older Mac, you'll likely have other applications that aren't included in this list (such as iLife).

Address Book

If you've used previous versions of OS X, the first time you launch Address Book you'll be in for a surprise. The program sports a completely new look in Lion: the old, utilitarian interface has been replaced by an interface that looks like an actual address book (Figure 6-1).

Figure 6-1. The new look of the venerable OS X Address Book

As with previous versions of OS X, Address Book keeps track of all your contacts' information—everything from phone numbers to email addresses. You can customize entries, so adding and deleting fields is no problem. To change the label for a field or add a completely new field for a contact, just click the Edit button at the bottom of the card. The best thing about Address Book is that it's integrated throughout Mac OS X, so you can access your contacts in Mail, iChat, and even some third-party applications.

While you can use the new version of Address Book in the same way you used older ones, this latest version offers some new functionality. You can initiate a FaceTime call, compose a letter, visit a contact's Facebook page, and much more. How? Just click on the label next to any bit of data (email, phone number, etc.) and hold down your mouse/trackpad button, and a menu will pop up showing you Address Book's brand-new options related to that piece of info (Figure 6-2).

Figure 6-2. Is there anything Address Book can't do?

NOTE

When you set up your Mac, Address Book automatically adds an entry for you. That might seem crazy—after all, you know how to get in touch with yourself—but there are benefits. For example, you can drag your card from Address Book into an email to send it to anyone you wish.

App Store

When Apple mentions "electronic distribution" while trumpeting the new features in Lion, what the company's really talking about is the Mac App Store. If you use an iOS device or if you've installed Lion on an older Mac, you're familiar with how the App Store operates.

For the uninitiated, there are a few things to remember. You log into the Mac App Store with either your iTunes account or

Apple ID. (Don't have an Apple ID? You can get one for free at *https://appleid.apple.com*.) Using the Mac App Store differs from the traditional way you're used to managing software. Instead of having to search for updates, you'll find any updates to your purchases prominently indicated in the App Store; click Updates to install the latest versions of all your purchases. You can install App Store purchases on any of your authorized Macs (up to five).

NOTE

You can't authorize or deauthorize machines via the Mac App Store. Instead, you have to open iTunes, click its Store drop-down menu, and then manage authorized Macs from there using the Authorize/Deauthorize This Computer commands.

Automator

Automator is a workflow tool for automating repetitive tasks: resizing photos, converting file types, combining text files, syncing files between folders—that kind of thing. In Lion, Automator looks and acts much like previous versions, and at first glance you won't notice the difference. But closer inspection reveals new actions that make automating things even easier. So if there was something you couldn't get Automator to do before, now is a great time to revisit this application. Automator now also supports Auto Save and Versions (see "Auto Save and Versions" on page 12), as well as workflow conversions.

Still not finding the script you need? Google has you covered: type "automator actions" into the Google search box and you'll find scads of prewritten scripts.

Calculator

When you fire up this application, you get a basic calculator. If you explore the program's menu bar, you'll note that it has built-in conversion functions, scientific and programmer modes (in the View menu), and numerous conversion functions (in the Convert menu). If you want a history of your calculations, you can get a running record by using Paper Tape (⌘-T). Calculator can also speak: the program can announce both button presses and your results; just visit the Speech menu in Calculator's menu bar.

NOTE

Using Calculator for basic math isn't the fastest way to get the answer—Spotlight can do math, too. So if you need a simple expression calculated, type it into Spotlight (see Figure 6-3) and skip Calculator altogether!

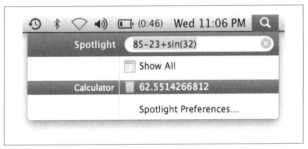

Figure 6-3. The same answer as Calculator, but much more convenient

Chess

Fancy a game of chess? If so, Mac OS X has you covered. Predictably, you get the standard human-versus-computer chess game (with adjustable difficulty), but you also get four chess variants, a tweakable board and pieces, and the ability to speak to your Mac to move pieces. (If you don't like the default view, you can change the tilt of the chessboard by clicking and holding the mouse button anywhere on the board's border. Arrows will pop up that allow you to tilt and rotate the board to your liking.)

You can also pit the computer against itself or play against another human. Sadly, you can't play chess against someone over a network, so if you want a head-on challenge with a human, they'll have to be at your Mac with you. Any time you want to save your game, just hit ⌘-S (Auto Save isn't implemented in Chess yet).

Dashboard

The Dashboard icon in the Applications folder simply launches Dashboard, but there are better ways of launching it than that. You can use the Dashboard gesture (see "Multitouch trackpads" on page 139), the keyboard shortcut (F4), or Mission Control. For more on this feature, see "The Dashboard" on page 87.

Dictionary

This is the dictionary responsible for Mac OS X's system-wide spellcheck. When you mistype a word, the suggested spelling will appear beneath the word (just like on iOS devices); hit Return to accept the suggestion (don't worry—pressing Return won't add a paragraph break to your document) or just keep typing and OS X will insert the suggestion for you. If you're not happy with OS X's suggestion you can click the tiny ×. For spelling (like mine) that's so bad OS X can't even guess at the word you want, you'll get a dashed red line under the word mocking your ineptitude. Right-click or Control-click words underlined in red to see your Mac's suggestions. If you hate your words being corrected automatically, visit the Language & Text preference pane (see "Language & Text" on page 123) and, on the Text tab, uncheck "Correct spelling automatically."

The Dictionary application is more than just a spellchecker. It also lets you search the *New Oxford English Dictionary*, the

Oxford American Writer's Thesaurus, Apple's dictionary, and Wikipedia. You can choose which of these four options to use, or search them all at the same time, by clicking the appropriate word near the top of the window (All, Dictionary, and so on). Dictionary is a global application, so you can use it to look up definitions anywhere on your Mac. To do so, select the word in question and then either right-click or Control-click the word and choose Look Up "[word]," or use a three-finger double-tap if you have a trackpad capable of understanding that gesture.

DVD Player

DVD Player plays (surprise!) DVDs. If you're upset that Front Row (the program that made video and picture viewing more comfortable in previous versions of OS X) isn't included in Lion, you'll be pleased to learn that DVD Player is a full-screen app, so you can still get that immersive viewing experience when you're watching something intense like *Chairman of the Board*. DVD Player also includes many options that let you do things like tweak the color or mess with the audio equalizer. And if you've got an Apple remote lying around, you can use it to control DVD Player.

NOTE

By default, DVD Player fires up the movie in Full Screen mode (you can change this behavior by selecting DVD Player→Preferences). Move your mouse to the bottom of the screen to access the playback controls; to the top of the screen to select a chapter; and to the *very* top of the screen to reveal the menu bar, where you can change the size of the playback window.

FaceTime

You've been able to video chat with a Mac since Apple introduced iSight and iChat AV, so what's the big deal with Face-

---

Time on a Mac? FaceTime does something iChat can't do: it lets you chat *face-to-face* (of course) with iOS aficionados and others other running Lion.

When you first launch FaceTime, you'll be greeted by Preferences in the sidebar. Decide which email address you want to receive FaceTime calls at, hit Done, and the Preferences sidebar will be replaced by a scrollable list of your contacts. Click on the person you want to contact and decide if you want to contact her iOS device (iPhone 4 or iPad 2 or newer) or her Mac. For iPads and Macs, you use an email address that the person's set (click it!); for iPhone calls, you can just click on the number.

WARNING

If you haven't visited the Mail, Contacts & Calendars preference pane yet, you'll have to create an Apple ID or use one you already have to get going with FaceTime.

Font Book

Font Book gives you control over all the fonts on your Mac. Lion installs over 100 fonts by default and other programs may install even more. You can preview, group, install, and deactivate fonts using Font Book. This program is also happy to validate your fonts (go to File→Validate Font) to identify any damaged ones that might cause your system to become unstable. In some cases, duplicate copies of fonts can also cause programs to become unstable. Font Book lets you deactivate duplicate fonts: go to Edit→Look for Duplicates. If Font Book finds duplicates, you'll have the choice of resolving them manually or automatically.

iCal

iCal has been the standard OS X calendaring app since Panther (10.3). The version of iCal that comes with Lion (5.0) is a substantial departure from previous versions. Its look now closely mimics a desktop blotter. You can run iCal in Full Screen mode, which is particularly handy when looking at a full year of entries and checking out another new feature of iCal: the heat map. iCal automatically assigns colors that reflect your availability on a particular day; the more cluttered your schedule, the redder the day will be.

The handiest new feature is the Quick Event button (the + in the upper left of the iCal window): click it, type in a phrase like "meeting 9 on Monday," and iCal adds that event to your calendar. Don't worry: while iCal looks dramatically different in Lion, it still lets you do all the same calendaring tasks you did in previous versions.

iChat

iChat is an instant-messaging system and a little more. It lets you have a text, audio, or video chat with another user (AIM and Jabber chat servers are supported, as well), but you can also show off your pictures with a slideshow or give a Keynote presentation. You can even set up conferences and have the participants chat with one another. iChat also offers the ability to share screens, which is a great way to troubleshoot a friend's or relative's Mac. And in Lion, iChat has been upgraded to include a full-screen mode, the ability to connect with Yahoo! Messenger users, and support for (and protection from) third-party plug-ins.

WARNING

If you're sharing your screen with another user, be aware that he or she can make changes, copy files, and delete things on your Mac, just as you do when you're using it.

Image Capture

Image Capture lets your Mac transfer images from a camera or a scanner. This is useful if you have a bunch of images you need to import from a device to some place other than iPhoto (which can import images, too).

iTunes

iTunes started out life as a way to manage the music you ripped from your CD library. It is a lot more than that now. iTunes lets you buy music, buy TV shows, rent or buy movies, and, almost incidentally, manage your music, TV shows, podcasts, movies, and iPhone/iPad/iPod Touch App Store purchases. It is also where you control the authorization of your Macs for the Mac App Store.

Launchpad

This application launcher and file-management system is covered in Chapter 1, see "Launchpad" on page 8.

Mail

Mail has been reimagined in Lion (see "Mail" on page 14 for more details). The layout has been radically changed (something you can undo by heading to Mail→Preferences→Viewing and then checking the "Use classic layout" box). Mail now uses a widescreen layout and organizes your emails into conversations. Like other Lion applications, Mail also received the full-screen treatment, so you can really expand your mail-reading real estate by going to View→Enter Full Screen or clicking the double arrows in the window's upper right (press Esc to exit Full Screen mode).

Mail is the standard email client for Mac OS X. It lets you set up rules to handle incoming messages, sending them directly to a destination folder depending on the criteria you select (go to Mail→Preferences→Rules). But there's more to Mail than just sending and receiving email. You can use it as your RSS reader and as a place to store notes for yourself; it even lets you create to-dos that include an alarm.

For good or ill, you can also create fancy email with Mail by using stationery templates. To access them, click the Stationery icon at the top right of any New Message window. Choose one and your mail will be full of color (and probably annoyance) for all the readers of your missive. If you're looking for an easy method of attaching photos (or using them with stationery), Mail includes a browser for all your images stored in iPhoto. In the New Message window, just click the Photo Browser icon (it's to the left of the Stationery icon) and choose the picture you want to attach. You can set up Smart Mailboxes that sort your email for you. The following sections contain more info on using Mail.

Adding new accounts

When you first run Mail, it will ask for your name, an existing email address, and the password for that account. (To add another account, select File→Add Account.) Type in those three bits of information and Mail will try to figure out how to configure your email server. If it can't, it'll ask you to provide detailed settings, such as the incoming server name, account type, and more. You can get that info from your administrator or Internet Service Provider.

NOTE

If you're just adding an email-only account, Mail is the way to go. But adding accounts with Mail isn't your best option if you're *also* using other services (like chat, calendaring, etc.) offered by your email provider. In that case, head to the Mail, Contacts & Calendar preference pane to take care of everything at once.

Some email services, such as Gmail, allow you to access your mail using either POP (Post Office Protocol) or IMAP (Internet Mail Access Protocol). If you like to access the same mail from multiple devices (such as an iPhone and a computer), IMAP is your best choice, because that way all your mail is stored on the server; when you read a message, it's marked as read across all the devices you access it from. (Some services may *require* you to enable IMAP before you can access them.) To enable IMAP for a service such as Gmail, log into your account using a web browser, and then visit the service's settings page. You may also need to look on the mail service's settings screen or in its help system for instructions on configuring Mail to access it via IMAP.

Add a signature to outgoing mail

If you end all your emails with the same thing (even if it's only "Thanks, Chris"), all that typing gets repetitive. You can use a signature to automatically append text or add a picture to the end of your messages.

To add a signature, go to Mail→Preferences→Signatures, and then, in the list on the left, choose the account you want to add a signature to (or choose All Signatures to create one for *all* your accounts). Click the + button and then type the signature text into the right-hand box (Mail automatically suggests your name and email address, but you can just type over that). If you want to use an image (such as a picture of your *actual* signature), scan it in, whittle it down to a small size (you can use Preview to do that), and drag the image into the right-hand box. If you add more than one signature, you can click the drop-down menu next to Choose Signature and specify a signature or tell Mail to rotate through your signatures sequentially or randomly.

Enable junk mail filtering

Head to Mail→Preferences→Junk Mail, and then make sure the box next to "Enable junk mail filtering" is checked. You can have Mail move the suspected junk to the Junk mailbox or leave it in your inbox. Note that every time you mark a message as junk, Mail learns from your action and improves its junk filtering. Mail's junk filter isn't 100 percent accurate, so if all your mail providers have their own server-side junk filtering, you might not want to bother with Lion's junk mail filtering.

Manage mailboxes

To add a new, standard mailbox, go to Mailbox→New Mailbox. To add a Smart Mailbox—which lets you set criteria for messages that should go straight into it (without you having to lift a finger)—choose New Smart Mailbox instead; you'll be presented with a window where you can set up your criteria.

Quickly delete junk mail

If you've become confident in Mail's ability to figure out which mail is junk, you can get rid of those messages by pressing Option-⌘-J or going to Mailbox→Erase Junk Mail.

Search your mail

You can use Spotlight to search for that elusive memo you want to reread, but if you use the search box in Mail's menu bar, you won't have to wade through search results from other sources. You'll get the same lightning-fast results, but you'll see only matches from your email, notes, and to-dos.

Mission Control

Mission Control earns a spot in the Applications folder and you can (obviously) launch it by clicking its icon there. For more info, see "Mission Control" on page 6.

Photo Booth

Photo Booth is likely the silliest and most fun application included with Lion. With PhotoBooth, you can do things as simple as snapping a picture with your Mac's built-in iSight camera and as complicated as filming a short movie with a fake background. PhotoBooth even allows you to trim clips by picking the starting and ending frames. Adding to the fun are the new effects included in this version and the ability to add your own backgrounds.

Preview

Preview is the default image viewer for Macs. Any image you download in a common format such as *.jpg*, *.png*, or *.pdf* will open in Preview by default. Preview lets you resize, crop, and annotate images and adjust their colors. You can also use Preview to snap screenshots, create icons, and more.

The version of Preview that ships with Lion offers a lot of improvements over the last version. For example, it now features support for Auto Save and Versions so you don't have to worry about losing your work. It also includes a Full Screen mode so you can maximize the pictures and PDFs you're editing.

QuickTime Player

QuickTime is the technology behind much of Mac OS X's media savvy: DVD Player, iTunes, and other applications rely heavily on it. You can use QuickTime Player to watch movies and listen to music. It's also useful for generating quick audio or visual content. You can record directly into QuickTime via your iSight camera, attached webcam, or microphone, and use the program to perform simple trimming. Once you've created something you want to share with the world, you can post it directly from QuickTime to a variety of destinations via the Share menu.

There's one other killer feature in QuickTime: the ability to record your screen. Choose File→New Screen Recording, click the red circle in the middle of the window that appears, and you'll be off to the wonderful world of screencasting.

Safari

Safari is the slick web browser that comes with Mac OS X. It includes a few new features in Lion: you can go full screen for immersive web browsing; there's a Reading List so you can mark longish articles for later perusal (click the eyeglasses icon at the left end of the toolbar); and a new downloads button on

---

the right side of the toolbar lets you see how downloads are progressing.

Even with these changes, Safari is still the browser you're used to. It's built on the open source WebKit browser platform (*http://webkit.org*), and it is both web standards–compliant and full-featured. There's a lot to Safari: it does everything you expect from a web browser and a little more, so getting it set up the way you want it is worth the effort.

Change the home page

When you get a new Mac, the default home page is *http://www .apple.com*. This is great if you love to keep up with Apple, but probably a bit boring for everyday use. To set a new home page, go to Safari→Preferences→General, and then type the URL of the page you want in the Homepage text box or, if you've already loaded the page you want, click "Set to Current Page."

Change the default browser

If you'd like to use a browser other than Safari (such as Firefox) by default, head to Safari→Preferences→General, and then choose the browser you want from the "Default web browser" pop-up menu.

Control which pages are shown in Top Sites

Safari 5 features a slick splash page, Top Sites, that includes snapshots of your most commonly visited sites. (To see it, either press Shift-⌘-1 or click the icon below the left side of the address bar that looks like a bunch of tiny squares.) It's useful and visually appealing, but Safari might put some pages there that you don't want to see. You can edit which pages are shown by clicking the Edit button in the lower-left corner of the Top Sites screen. Lock down pages you want to keep by clicking their pushpin icons, and banish pages you don't want shown by clicking their ×s. (A blue star in the corner of a web page means that the page has been updated since your last visit.)

You can add a page directly to Top Sites by choosing Bookmark→Add Bookmark and then choosing Top Sites from the menu that appears. (Note that Top Sites bookmarks aren't synced to MobileMe or iCloud, so you should save the URL somewhere in your Bookmarks Bar or Bookmarks menu, as well.)

Find a page you didn't bookmark

It happens to everyone: you see an interesting site but don't bother to bookmark it, and then three days later you want to go back to that site but don't remember what it's called or how you ended up on it. Safari's browsing history to the rescue! To bring up your history, select History→Show All History. Then type whatever snippet you remember about the mystery site in the Search box (the one below the Google search box). Safari returns all the web pages that you've been to that contain what you searched for.

Block pop-up ads

To enable pop-up blocking, go to Safari→Block Pop-Up Windows (Shift-⌘-K). A checkmark next to that menu item indicates the pop-up blocker is active.

Change where downloaded items are saved

By default, Safari saves downloaded items in the Downloads folder in your Home directory, but you can have Safari download to any spot you like. Go to Safari→Preferences→General tab, and then, in the "Save downloaded files to" pop-up menu, click Other and choose a new location.

Control cookies

Most websites send cookies (small bundles of data that are stored between sessions and visits to a website) to your browser. If you're concerned about how cookies are used, you can customize the way Safari handles them. Click Safari→Preferences→Privacy, and then choose the setting you want in the "Block cookies" section. You can also examine all the cookies that Safari has by clicking Details. From there, you can search, view, and remove cookies. To remove all cookies in one fell swoop, click Remove All Website Data.

Get rid of Safari's history

You might find yourself on sites that you don't really want to be on, but Safari isn't picky and saves *all* the sites you visit in its history. Although there are some things that, once seen, cannot be unseen, you may still like to pretend that you never visited a particular site. If so, you can either delete Safari's entire history (go to History→Clear History) or delete offending entries by hand (go to History→Show All History, select the site(s) you want to get rid of, and then hit the Delete key).

If you do nothing, Safari will still delete your browsing history after one month. If this interval is too long or too short for your taste, you can change its duration by adjusting Safari's preferences. Take a trip to Safari→Preferences→General and change the "Remove history items" setting. You can choose preset intervals between one day and one year or take control of the situation and select Manually.

Add a URL to the desktop

If you like to have sites you frequently visit accessible directly from the desktop, highlight the URL of the site you want in Safari's address bar and then drag the URL directly onto the desktop. Alternatively, you can drag a site's favicon (the icon to the left of the page's address) instead. Either way, a file icon (which looks like a piece of paper with a giant @ on it) appears on your desktop with the URL or page's title as its name. Now you can double-click this icon to load that page in your default browser. To change the name of the icon, single-click its name and then type something more meaningful, just as you would with any other file.

Browse privately

There are times when you don't want Safari keeping track of your history; Private Browsing is the answer. To turn it on, click Safari→Private Browsing. The dialog box that appears details what Private Browsing does. Click OK to browse without having search box searches remembered, sites you visit added to Safari's history, or cookies stored permanently.

WARNING

Private Browsing isn't a "set it and forget it" option; it applies to your current session only. So if you quit Safari, the next time you open it, Private Browsing will be inactive and Safari will diligently record all of your online comings and goings.

Make Safari remember passwords for website logins

This is a great timesaver, although it's a bit of a security risk if you leave your Mac unattended while you're logged in (for a tip on making that a little safer, see "Password Management" on page 190). To get Safari to remember and automatically enter your login information for websites, go to Safari→Preferences→AutoFill, and check the box next to "User names and passwords." From then on, when you enter a username and password into a site, Safari will ask if you want to save it. (You may find that some sites, especially banking and credit card sites, don't allow you to save passwords.)

Use a different default RSS reader

Safari is the default RSS reader in Mac OS X, but you might prefer to use Mail or a third-party RSS reader such as NetNewsWire. To make this change, you can go to Safari→Preferences→RSS, and then select the RSS reader of your choice from the "Default RSS reader" pop-up menu.

Customize Safari's toolbar

Safari's default toolbar is missing some buttons you might want, such as a Home button to take you to your home page. You can add buttons to Safari's toolbar by going to View→Customize Toolbar and then dragging the buttons you want right onto the toolbar. While the Customize Toolbar pane is open, you can also get rid of the things you don't want on Safari's toolbar by dragging them off of it, and rearrange toolbar items by dragging them around.

Stickies

Stickies are a virtual version of Post-it notes. Fire up this application and you can leave notes all over your desktop. Select File→New or press ⌘-N to create a blank note you can type in, add images to, and use for reminders. When the list on a sticky becomes something you need to share, you can export it as rich text by choosing File→Export Text.

System Preferences

This is the place to tweak Mac OS X. System Preferences are covered in Chapter 5.

TextEdit

TextEdit is a not-too-shabby word processor that you can use to write the great American novel or a grocery list. Although earlier versions of TextEdit were limited, it keeps gaining features in every new version of Mac OS X. For example, TextEdit takes advantage of Auto Save and Versions. Lion's system-wide spellchecker is available in the program, and you can also add a grammar check (select TextEdit→Preferences and turn on "Check grammar with spelling"). TextEdit's default format for saving files is *.rtf* (Rich Text Format), but you can also save (and open) HTML; OpenOffice.org (*.odt*); and Microsoft Word 97, 2003, and 2007 documents. TextEdit can also open and save *.docx* (Word 2011) files, but you'll likely lose some formatting when you open one; saving as a *.docx* file preserves the formatting from TextEdit.

NOTE

You can even add text styles in TextEdit: select some text and then use the Format menu to make it look the way you want. Then click the Styles button at the top left of the editing window (the button has a ¶ symbol on it), choose Show Styles, and then click "Add to Favorites" (Figure 6-4). You'll then be able to give the file a name for future use.

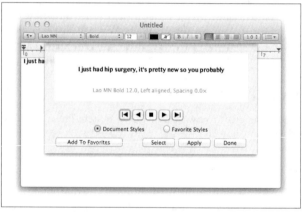

Figure 6-4. TextEdit styles in action

Time Machine

Time Machine automates the backing-up process and puts a beautiful graphical interface on flipping back time. To use Time Machine, all you really need is an attached drive with sufficient space, another Mac, or Time Capsule (Apple's all-in-one backup device and WiFi router).

Time Machine operates seamlessly once it's set up and turned on. To set it up, connect a suitable drive, and then launch Time Machine (Applications→Time Machine), click Set Up Time Machine, and then choose which disk (or Time Capsule) you want to use as a Time Machine disk. After Time Machine is up and running, you can make a few adjustments. When you launch Time Machine, you'll see a big On/Off button, a button to bring up the Select Disk dialog box, and an Options button. Clicking the Options button lets you specify which folders and drives you *don't* want backed up; just click the + button in the dialog box that appears and then select the items you want to exclude.

Using Time Machine is intuitive when you're looking for a file you accidentally deleted (click the Time Machine menu extra or application icon to launch Time Machine, and then navigate through the available backups). But if you want to restore your system from a Time Machine backup, you'll first need to boot from the Lion Recovery HD (see "Startup troubleshooting" on page 110). Once you've booted up and picked your installation language, don't start installing Mac OS X. Instead, click the menu bar and select Utilities. The last option in the drop-down menu is Restore System From Backup; selecting it lets you choose the Time Machine disk or Time Capsule you want to use to restore your system.

Utilities Included with Lion

What's the difference between an application and a utility? It's largely semantic. Utilities are a type of application. But in general, the ones called "applications" allow you to create and modify data, while the ones called "utilities" allow you to monitor and manage your Mac. There's a reason Utilities is a subfolder of Applications and not the other way around: utilities are usually not as exciting as the applications you find in the rest of the Applications folder.

But that doesn't mean the Utilities folder is full of arcane, boring stuff. There are plenty of useful applications inside. You'll imagine great uses for a lot of them once you get a quick peek at what they do.

Activity Monitor

The main window of Activity Monitor gives you a list of all the processes running on your Mac (click a column heading to change how the list is sorted). You can view stats about CPU load, system memory, disk activity, disk usage, or your network using the buttons near the bottom of the window. Click on a process and then click the Inspect icon to get a closer look at the process. You can also use Activity Monitor to quit any process by selecting the process and clicking the Quit Process icon (very useful when a program is needlessly hogging the processor or is unresponsive).

NOTE

If Activity Monitor is running, it displays a constantly running graph of system usage in the Dock. You can control what data is being displayed by right-clicking on the Dock icon and choosing the data you want Disk Utility to display in the Dock.

AirPort Utility

If you own a Time Capsule, an AirPort base station, or an AirPort Express, you can use this utility to manage those devices.

AppleScript Editor

AppleScript is a programming language that's designed to be easy to use. It can control scriptable applications on your Mac (that includes most, but not all, applications), allowing you to generate scripts that can, for example, resize photos automatically. Using the AppleScript Editor allows you to write, edit, test, run, and compile AppleScripts. For more information, see *http://developer.apple.com/applescript*.

Audio MIDI Setup

MIDI is an acronym for Musical Instrument Digital Interface. This utility lets you hook musical instruments up to your computer, which is useful for fans of GarageBand and other audio programs.

Bluetooth File Exchange

Use this utility to send files to supported Bluetooth devices, such as phones, PDAs, or other computers. (Bluetooth is slower than WiFi but requires less setup to transfer files.) After you launch this utility, you can either drag the file you want to transfer onto the Bluetooth Dock icon and wait for a list of recipients to appear, or select a file in the Bluetooth File Exchange window and then click the Send button (and wait for the list of possible recipients to appear).

Boot Camp Assistant

Boot Camp Assistant lets you install Windows (XP, Vista, or 7) on any Mac running Lion. This utility will partition your hard drive and install the necessary drivers. (Obviously, you'll need a Windows installation disk.) Once Boot Camp Assistant works its magic, you'll have a dual-boot Mac capable of running Lion or Windows. (You choose which operating system to boot into using the Startup Disk preference pane—see "Startup Disk" on page 155.)

ColorSync Utility

Because everyone sees colors a little differently and devices often interpret colors in different ways, ColorSync helps you manage colors. It lets you repair ICC (International Color Consortium) profiles on your Mac (click the Profile First Aid icon to do so). Click the Profiles icon to inspect the profiles used by your Mac; ColorSync displays a groovy 3-D plot of the profile you select (when applicable). The Devices icon lets you manage the profiles of attached devices. ColorSync Utility also allows you to apply filters to, for example, a PDF document with the Filters icon. Finally, the Calculator icon lets you sample any pixel displayed on your computer and find its values (click the magnifying glass icon and then click the color you're interested in).

Console

Unlike your car keys, your Mac keeps track of itself. Every time something unexpected (or even routine) happens, the system notes the problem in a log, but these logs are a bit difficult to find. That's where Console comes in: it lets you review the errors logged on your Mac much more conveniently than if you had to dig through the Library folder. Clicking on the Show Log List icon toggles a sidebar showing the logs available on your computer. The logs contain information critical for diagnosing bugs you send to Apple and can be useful in tracking a problematic application.

DigitalColor Meter

With this utility, you can inspect the color values of anything displayed on screen. You can set the size of the aperture (all the way down to a single pixel) and choose from four different ways the results can be calculated.

Disk Utility

Disk Utility is a toolbox for all your disks. You can use it to erase disks (including CD-RWs and DVD-RWs), format disks, mount and unmount disks (if you've ejected an attached disk, you can remount it without unplugging/replugging it by clicking Disk Utility's Mount icon), securely delete data, create compressed or uncompressed disk images, repair permissions, partition disks, and more. To learn how to use Disk Utility to check your drive's health, see the section "Startup Problems" on page 108.

Grab

Grab is Mac OS X's screen-capture utility. It lets you capture a section of the screen, a complete window (sans drop shadow), or the entire screen. It even has a timed option that gives you 10 seconds to get whatever process you're trying to capture running. All the images are saved in *.tiff* format.

Grapher

Grapher displays graphs of equations that are built into the program, as well as equations you enter. This utility can handle a wide range of coordinate choices (polar, cylindrical, Cartesian, and spherical), and can even generate 3-D graphs. This is a useful tool if you're studying calculus.

Java Preferences

This utility is where you tell your Mac what you want the Java programming language to do for you and how. It lets you select your preferred version of Java, manage security, and configure debugging.

Keychain Access

Keychain Access stores your passwords for the moments when you inevitably forget them. As long as you remember your system password, you can recover any password stored in the Keychain. (Many third-party programs, like Firefox, don't use Keychain.) You can also create secure notes readable only in Keychain that are locked with your password. For more on Keychain Access, see Chapter 7.

Migration Assistant

When you first set up your Mac, you had the option of transferring your data from another computer. You were also assured that if you didn't want to transfer your data right then, you could do it later. For more info on all the ways you can transfer data using Migration Assistant, see "Moving Data and Applications from Another Computer" on page 26.

Network Utility

Network Utility lets you perform common networking tasks. Most users will find the Info tab the most useful. For those familiar with Unix network diagnostics, there are also tabs for Netstat, Ping, Lookup, Traceroute, Whois, Finger, and Port Scan.

Podcast Capture

This app works with Podcast Producer, which comes with OS X Lion Server. The first thing the app will force you to do is to enter the name of the server you're going to use. If you don't have a server for Podcast Capture, the fun stops there. If you do have one, you can use this utility to record your screen, yourself, or audio and send it to the server where it can then be encoded and distributed.

Podcast Publisher

If you don't have OS X Lion Server and are jealous of the capabilities of Podcast Capture, don't worry—Podcast Publisher has you covered (Figure 6 5).

Podcast Publisher manages to do three distinct podcasting tasks in one slick program: create podcasts, archive episodes, and publish podcasts. (You'd expect that last feature based on this utility's name, but the other two functions should come as a pleasant surprise.)

Since Podcast Publisher performs three different (though related) functions and you might be only interested in one, here's a look at each feature.

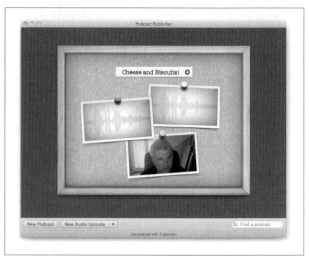

Figure 6-5. Brand new in Lion: Podcasting made easy!

Content Creation

There are a lot of ways to record audio and/or video with your Mac. You could use QuickTime, Photo Booth, or iMovie. With Podcast Publisher, you get a new choice: the utility has content-creation features built right in so you can create a podcast and publish it without even switching programs.

If it's your first time launching Podcast Publisher (or if you click New Podcast in the lower-left corner of the utility's window), you'll see a corkboard with a yellow sticky note imploring you to add a new episode. Before you crank out that first episode, give your podcast a cool name by clicking the generic name near the top of the window. Now it's time to create some content.

If you want to do a video podcast, click the "Add a new episode" sticky note. The window will change to the image from your iSight surrounded by a black border (you can use a different camera by visiting the Camera menu). At the bottom left of the window, you'll see a couple of unlabeled buttons. The button with the filmstrip on it is selected by default; if you want to record your desktop, click the button next to it.

Once you're ready to record, click the record button at the bottom center of the window. Sit through the three-second countdown and then record to your heart's content (you can switch between using the desktop recorder and iSight on the fly). When you're done recording, click the record button again. You'll then see a filmstrip or waveform representation of your creation under the main video area, allowing you to set when the episode starts and stops.

You might be wondering if you can do an audio-only podcast. But of course! On Podcast Publisher's main screen, simply click the triangle next to New Movie Episode and choose New Audio Episode. The recording process works exactly as described above, but only the audio from your Mac's built in mic will be recorded. (If you want to use a different mic, head to the Camera drop-down menu.)

Podcast Management

The editing powers of Podcast Publisher are severely limited, so you might not want to use it to create podcasts, but you may want to use it to *manage* your podcasts.

If you've created a podcast with some other program, you can import into Podcast Publisher. If it's in one of your media libraries, head to Podcast Publisher's View menu and choose Show Media Browser. Then drag the file over from the Media Browser and it will take a spot on Podcast Publisher's corkboard as a new episode. You can also drag and drop files from your Mac onto the corkboard to create new episodes. If your podcast resides on the Internet, you'll find an "Import Podcast from URL" option in the File menu.

With Podcast Publisher, you aren't limited to one podcast. You can have multiple podcasts, each with its own corkboard full of episodes. To create a distinct podcast, simply click the New Podcast button at the bottom of the window or press ⌘-N.

Once you've got enough podcasts and episodes sitting around to confuse yourself, you can clean things up. To delete a whole podcast, click a blank spot on its corkboard and then hit Delete. To delete an episode, click the virtual pushpin holding it to the virtual corkboard, and you'll get options to delete or get info about the episode. As you would expect, deleting something in Podcast Publisher only deletes it locally; if you've shared it, the episode or podcast will still be around.

Podcast Publishing

Podcast Publisher can manage and produce podcasts, but its name just wouldn't be appropriate if it couldn't help you publish podcasts, too. To publish a podcast, click the episode you want, and then click the Share button in the lower-right corner of the program's window. The first three options listed are for small-scale sharing: exporting the episode to iTunes (your local library), sending it with Mail, or generating a copy on your desktop. You'll also see options that let you share your podcast using a server or with a remote workflow.

RAID Utility

Got a RAID (Redundant Array of Inexpensive Disks) card installed in your Mac? No? Then you can ignore this utility. If you *do* have a RAID card, this utility lets you configure a RAID on your system.

System Information

This utility can tell you just about everything you might want to know about your Mac. Hardware, networks, and software are all covered in great detail. If you're wondering about any particular aspect of your Mac, System Information is the place to look.

There is some weirdness with System Information. If you invoke it by visiting the Utilities folder and double-clicking its icon, it will look just like System Profiler from Snow Leopard. This can be frustrating if you're looking for the new, more graphical display of system information. While all the info you need is available in the older-looking version of this utility, to get the graphical display shown in Figure 6-6, you have to invoke System Information by going to **⚫**→About This Mac→More Info.

Figure 6-6. Same utility, much cooler interface

Terminal

Mac OS X is built on Unix, and the Terminal utility is your window into that world. Unix is incredibly powerful and Terminal lets you run Unix commands. Clicking Help→Terminal Help will get you started if you aren't familiar with Unix. The most important Terminal tip? When you're confused, typing **man** *command-name* brings up a manual page where you can learn about a particular Unix command (try **man man** for starters). In Lion, Terminal gets a bit of an upgrade: it's now a full-screen application.

VoiceOver Utility

VoiceOver is Mac OS X's screen-reading program that describes what's happening on your screen using one of the voices installed with OS X. This utility allows you to customize VoiceOver's settings: you can control what voice is used, how your computer is navigated when using VoiceOver, how VoiceOver handles web pages, and how the keys on the keyboard control your Mac. You can even set up a Braille monitor. For additional information, flip to "Seeing tab" on page 129.

X11

X11 is the Mac OS X version of the X Window System, which allows your Mac to run many graphical Unix applications.

CHAPTER 7

Managing Passwords in Lion

When you first boot a new Mac and set up a user, the system is configured to automatically log in that user. That's probably fine if you're the only person who uses that Mac, but not so great if your Mac is sitting out where a lot of people have access to it. You'll want to customize your security settings to fit the environment where you'll be using your Mac. If it's a desktop machine and you'll only be using it at home, for example, you probably don't have much to worry about. But if it's a Mac-Book that you plan on hauling everywhere you go, you'll want a little more security.

NOTE

See "Logging In" on page 44 to find out how to disable automatic login. And see "Logging Out, Sleeping, and Shutting Down" on page 45 to customize your logout options.

Security in Mac OS X usually comes down to passwords: passwords for services, accounts, websites, and email. Once you've created all those pesky but necessary passwords, you'll want to turn your attention to managing them.

Password Management

To manage all your passwords, Lion uses keychains; they're where it stores your passwords and certificates to keep them safe from prying eyes. These keychains save you a lot of time, because your Mac can use the stored passwords to do a variety of useful things, like joining your wireless network without any help from you.

The more you do online, the more passwords you need. Ideally, you want different passwords for everything; using the same password for your bank's website and for posting to a third-rate message board isn't the best idea. However, with so many passwords running around, it is easy to forget them. We've all been faced with the situation where we were *sure* we typed in the right password only to be repeatedly denied access. Fortunately, Mac OS X can help.

Recovering a Forgotten Password

So you've forgotten the password to some rarely visited yet essential server or some network you only join every six months. Turns out Lion probably remembered the password for you (to have it save website passwords, too, see "Make Safari remember passwords for website logins" on page 174). To recover the password, open Keychain Access (Applications→Utilities→Keychain Access) and type the name of the site, application, or something relevant into the program's search box. Keychain Access will find entries that match your search criteria and present you with a list like the one in Figure 7-1.

When whatever you're looking for appears in the list in the middle of the Keychain Access window, double-click that item's name and a window will pop up that includes a "Show password" checkbox. Check the box, enter your Mac OS X password, and you'll see the password.

Figure 7-1. Recovering my Safari Books Online password

NOTE

For an added level of security, you can configure Mac OS X to lock your keychain after a period of inactivity. Open Keychain Access, click "login" in the Keychains list on the left side of the window, and then select Edit→"Change Settings for Keychain 'login.'" You'll then be able to lock the keychain after a period of inactivity or when the computer sleeps. Once a keychain is locked, Lion won't let your Mac give out passwords until you unlock the keychain by typing in your password.

Make a Great Password

The following passwords are not acceptable: *letmein*, *password*, *123*, and *qwerty*. Using one of those for anything you care about is like leaving the door to your house wide open—but removing the welcome mat. Sure, a miscreant *might* pause momentarily when he notices the welcome mat is missing, but that won't stop him from coming into your house. You need a better password.

Lion can help you in your quest. You can find out whether your chosen password is strong with Password Assistant, which tests the strength of your password. For whatever reason, you can't access Password Assistant directly, so you'll have to use

Keychain Access to get to it. (Actually, any prompt that displays the little key icon will give you access to Password Assistant, but Keychain Access is one of the easiest ways to get there.) Open Keychain Access (Applications→Utilities→Keychain Access), and then select Edit→"Change Password for Keychain '[keychain name].'"

NOTE

There is an excellent free utility that will invoke Password Assistant any time you want to generate a new password. To get a copy, point your browser to *http://www.codepoetry.net/products/passwordassistant*.

In the "Enter a new password for keychain '[keychain name]'" dialog box that pops up, type a prospective password in the New Password field. As you type, you'll see a colored bar appear that indicates how good your password is (red for weak, yellow for fair, and green for good or excellent). Under that is a Password Strength rating (Weak, Fair, Good, or Excellent). When you're done typing, click the key icon and the Password Assistant window appears (Figure 7-2).

If your password isn't the digital equivalent of Fort Knox, try out some new passwords to see how they rate. If you can't come up with a good one on your own, Lion is happy to pitch in and help. The Tips field gives you pointers on how to build a better password, and the Type drop-down menu lets you choose the kinds of passwords Lion suggests: "memorable" ones, ones with letters and numbers, purely numeric ones, random ones, or FIPS-181-compliant ones (the kind used by government agencies).

Once you've found a good, strong password, close the Password Assistant window and then click Cancel in the "Enter a new password for..." window (unless you actually want to change the password for that keychain). Now you can type that password into whatever program or website needs it and know that your info should be pretty secure.

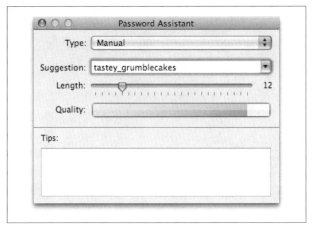

Figure 7-2. Know your password's strength

Storing Secure Notes

Keychain is great at storing passwords, but you can also use it to store notes. To write a note that no one else can see (well, except for people who know your username and password), open Keychain Access (Applications→Utilities→Keychain Access), click "login" in the Keychains list, select Secure Notes in the Category section, and then click the + button at the bottom of the window. Give your secret note a name and then start typing away (Figure 7 3). When you're done, click Add and your note will be safely stored in the Keychain.

Add a Keychain Access Menu Extra

With all the goodness Keychain Access offers, you might want easy access to it. You can add it to your Dock, but that might be getting a little crowded, and the Keychain icon isn't the best-looking one Apple has churned out. Luckily, you can add a menu extra for Keychain Access (see "Menu extras" on page 55 for a refresher). To do that, the next time you're using Keychain Access, go to Preferences (⌘-,) and in

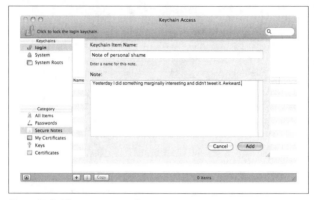

Figure 7-3. They must never know

the General tab, check the box next to "Show keychain status in menu bar."

Securing Your Data

Carefully choosing passwords is a great start when it comes to security, but it's not a perfect solution. If someone has physical access to your Mac, there are things she can do to get at your data. If this prospect seems particularly loathsome to you, you should consider making the extra effort to enable FileVault 2, a feature of Lion that makes your data impossible to access unless you want it accessed. For information on setting up FileVault 2, see "FileVault tab" on page 126.

CHAPTER 8

Keyboard Commands and Special Characters

When you're using the keyboard, you want to keep your hands on the keys. A trip to the mouse or hunting for a special character can really slow you down. The good news is that Lion has a lot of both key commands and special characters built right in. The bad news is that, unless you're one of those people who memorize the digits of pi to a thousand places for fun, you won't remember them all.

The most important key commands and special characters vary from user to user. For example, if you're writing about Exposé, knowing how to type é really helps, but knowing how to type ¬ isn't of much use. Everyone uses his or her Mac a little differently, so this chapter features a wide selection of keyboard commands and ways to type different characters. Memorize the ones for the functions you use most, and you'll save a lot of time and effort.

Key Commands

When your hands are on the keyboard, it's much quicker to keep them there to perform some mundane task than it is to dig through the menus and find the option that lets you type a special character or create a new folder.

In general, the less time you spend using the mouse (or track-pad), the more productive you'll be when using the keyboard. While you'll want to learn the keyboard commands for all your favorite programs, some commands are so common that it's worth reserving a special spot for them in your brain:

⌘-S

> Save. This saves the document you're working on. The more often you use this command, the happier you'll be (at least until Lion's Auto Save feature is uniformly implemented). Nothing is more frustrating than having all your hard work disappear when the power flickers or an application crashes.

NOTE

If you're using a keyboard designed for Windows systems, you won't see the ⌘ key. Instead, use the Windows key, which is usually in the same spot you'd find the ⌘ key. Some keyboards use a different symbol, however; for example, the Happy Hacking Keyboard uses the "lozenge" symbol (◊).

⌘-C

> Copy. This command copies the current selection for later pasting.

⌘-V

> Paste. Once you've copied something, you'll want to paste it.

⌘-X

> Cut. This command deletes the current selection but copies it to your Mac's memory. After you've cut something, you can paste it elsewhere until you copy or cut something else.

⌘-,

> Opens the preferences for the active application.

⌘-] and ⌘-[

> Moves forward (]) and backwards ([) in the Finder, Safari, and some other applications.

⌘-Shift-?

> Opens the current application's Help dialog box so you can get quick answers to your vexing questions.

⌘-Q

> Quits the current application.

NOTE

> You can't easily quit the Finder, so this command doesn't work when you're using it. To find out how to quit the Finder (well, to relaunch it), see "The Finder stops responding" on page 101.

⌘-Tab

> This command brings up the application switcher, which lets you cycle through running applications by pressing Tab repeatedly as you hold down ⌘. When you get to the application you're after, let go of both keys. If your hands are on the keyboard, this is a *much* faster way to switch applications than the Dock.

Option-⌘-Esc

> Force quits the current program.

Once you've mastered those commands, your appetite for keyboard shortcuts is likely to become insatiable. Fortunately, there's plenty more of that keyboard-shortcut, time-saving goodness, much of which is shown in Table 8-1.

Unfortunately, some of these commands aren't supported uniformly across all programs. For example, in the
Finder and many other applications, ⌘-I displays the Get
Info dialog box for the currently selected file or object,
but in most word-processing applications, ⌘-I italicizes
the selected text.

Also, on some keyboards, you may need to hold down
the key labeled Fn to use keyboard shortcuts that require
a function key (F1, F2, etc.).

Table 8-1. Common keyboard shortcuts

Key command	Most common action	Finder action
⌘-A	Selects all	Selects all items in current directory
⌘-B	Makes selected text bold (in word-processing programs).	None
⌘-C	Copies current selection	Copies selected files and folders
⌘-D	Duplicates selected object (usually in drawing applications)	Duplicates selected file or folder
⌘-E	Searches for highlighted text	Ejects disk
⌘-F	Finds text	Opens a new Finder window with cursor in search field
⌘-H	Hides current application	Hides Finder
⌘-I	Italicizes selected text	Opens Get Info window for selected item
⌘-J	Jumps to currently selected text (useful if you've selected some text, then scrolled elsewhere in a document)	Shows View options

Key command	Most common action	Finder action
⌘-K	Clears screen (Terminal) or inserts hyperlink (text editors, word processors, and Mail)	Opens "Connect to Server" window
⌘-L	Goes to line number (common in text editors)	Creates an alias
⌘-M	Minimizes window	Same
⌘-N	Creates new document	Opens new Finder window
⌘-O	Displays Open File dialog box	Opens selected item
⌘-P	Prints	None
⌘-Q	Quits current application	None
⌘-R	Varies	Shows original file when an alias is selected
⌘-S	Saves current file	None
⌘-T	Displays Font panel	Adds selected item to Finder window sidebar
⌘-V	Pastes copied item	Pastes copied file(s) or folder(s)
⌘-W	Closes window	Same
⌘-X	Cuts	None
⌘-Z	Undoes most recent action	Same
⌘-1	Varies	Displays Finder items as icons
⌘-2	Varies	Displays Finder items as list
⌘-3	Varies	Displays Finder items as columns
⌘-4	Varies	Displays Finder items in Cover Flow View
⌘-Delete	Varies	Moves selected item to Trash
⌘-Tab	Opens Application Switcher	Same
⌘-[	Goes back (when using a web browser)	Goes back one directory

Key command	Most common action	Finder action
⌘-]	Goes forward (when using a web browser)	Goes forward one directory
⌘-?	Activates Help menu	Same
⌘-Space	Activates Spotlight search	Same
⌘-`	Cycles through application windows	Cycles through Finder windows
Tab	Moves focus to next item or (in text editors) inserts a tab	Moves focus to next item
Shift-⌘-3	Takes a picture of your screen; saves image file to desktop	Same
Shift-⌘-4	Displays a cursor for taking a snapshot of part of the screen (press Space to take a picture of a single window); saves image file to desktop	Same
Shift-Control-⌘-3	Works like ⌘-Shift-3, but copies picture to clipboard	Same
Shift-Control-⌘-4	Works like ⌘-Shift-4, but copies picture to clipboard	Same
Shift-⌘-A	Varies	Opens Applications folder
Shift-⌘-C	Varies	Opens Computer folder
Shift-⌘-D	Varies	Opens Desktop folder
Shift-⌘-O	Varies	Opens Documents folder
Shift-⌘-G	Varies	Opens "Go to the folder" dialog box
Shift-⌘-H	Varies	Opens Home folder
Shift-⌘-K	Varies	Opens Network folder
Shift-⌘-N	Varies	Creates a new folder
Shift-⌘-Q	Displays logout dialog box, logs out automatically after one minute	Same
Shift-⌘-S	Opens "Save As..." dialog box	None
Shift-⌘-U	Varies	Opens Utilities folder

Key command	Most common action	Finder action
Shift-⌘-Delete	Varies	Opens Empty Trash dialog box
Shift-Option-⌘-Delete	Varies	Empties Trash
Option (while dragging)	Copies item to new location	Copies file/folder to new location
⌘-Option (while dragging)	Varies	Creates an alias to a file/folder at new location
Option-⌘-D	Shows or hides the Dock	Same
Option-⌘-M	Varies	Minimizes all windows
Option-⌘-Esc	Forces an application to quit	Same
Option-⌘-Eject	Puts computer to sleep	Same
Control-Eject	Displays the Restart/Sleep/Shut Down dialog box	Same
Control-⌘-Eject	Quits all applications and restarts computer	Same

You're probably not going to remember *all* of those shortcuts, but you'll likely remember the ones you use frequently. And more time at the keyboard means less time wasted mousing and searching for commands.

Customizing Key Commands

If you don't like the key commands built into Mac OS X, you don't have to put up with them. You can change them or add your own by taking a trip to the Keyboard preference pane. For details, see "Keyboard Shortcuts tab" on page 135.

Typing Special Characters in Mac OS X

If you're banging away on the keyboard and find yourself wanting to type special characters (like the é in Exposé, for example), there are convoluted methods of getting the character you want (pasting them from the Web, say), but you might be wondering if there's a trackpadless or mouse-free way to do it. In Lion, there is.

One of the underrated new features of Lion is an easy way to get at those pesky diacritic symbols. Simply type the letter you're interested in and *hold the key down*, and a window will pop up with all your options (as in Figure 8-1). You can then use the arrow keys to select the diacritic you want, or press the number key that corresponds to the number below your pick.

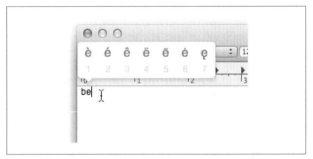

Figure 8-1. All your options for e

This new feature is universal, so you can use it anywhere you can type a character. It does have a couple of drawbacks, though: depending on how your key repeat rate is set, you might find yourself typing *sss* before the diacritic menu shows up, and if you type a special character often, you'll want to commit its keyboard shortcut to memory to save yourself some time.

Table 8-2 shows how to easily type diacritic symbols.

Table 8-2. Diacritic accent mark shortcuts

Symbol	Name	Keystroke
´	Acute	Option-E, then type the letter
^	Circumflex	Option-I, then type the letter
`	Grave	Option-`, then type the letter
~	Tilde	Option-N, then type the letter
¨	Umlaut	Option-U, then type the letter

That takes care of only a few characters you may not be able to find on your keyboard. But what about other characters, such as the euro symbol or the Apple logo? You might try looking through the Font Book utility, but with the number of fonts included in a standard OS X install, that task can require more luck than skill.

The Character Palette is a bit easier to use. You enable it by heading to Applications→System Preferences→Language & Text. Click the Input Sources tab, and then check the box labeled Keyboard & Character Viewer. Your Mac adds a new icon to the left side of the menu bar that lets you launch either Character Viewer or Keyboard Viewer. Character Viewer lets you browse a wide variety of special characters and insert them into documents by clicking them (the characters appear in the most recently used application). With Keyboard Viewer (Figure 8-2), you can hold down Shift, Option, or Shift *and* Option simultaneously to see how the keyboard is modified when you're depressing those modifier keys. As with Character Viewer, you can click the letters or symbols to insert them into a text field.

Figure 8-2. Wonder what Option+Shift does to the characters on your keyboard? Wonder no more!

You can also check out Table 8-3 for a quick reference to U.S. English keyboard modifiers.

Table 8-3. Special character shortcuts for U.S. English keyboards

No modifiers	Shift	Option	Shift-Option
`	~	` (above next vowel typed)	`
1	!	¡	(fraction slash symbol)
2	@	™	€
3	#	£	‹
4	$	¢	›
5	%	∞	fi (ligature)
6	∧	§	fl (ligature)
7	&	¶	‡
8	*	•	°
9	(	a	•
0	)	o	‚
-	–	–	—
=	+	≠	±
q	Q	Œ	Œ

No modifiers	Shift	Option	Shift-Option
w	W	Σ	„
e	E	´ (above next vowel typed)	´
r	R	®	‰
t	T	†	ˇ
y	Y	¥	Á
u	U	¨ (above next vowel typed)	¨
i	I	^ (above next vowel typed)	^
o	O	ø	Ø
p	P	π	∏
[	{	"	"
]	}	'	'
\	|	«	»
a	A	å	Å
s	S	ß	Í
d	D	∂	Î
f	F	ƒ	Ï
g	G	©	"
h	H	·	Ó
j	J	Δ	Ô
k	K	°	
l	L	¬	Ò
;	:	…	Ú
'	"	Æ	Æ
z	Z	Ω	¸
x	X	≈	˛
c	C	ç	Ç

No modifiers	Shift	Option	Shift-Option
v	V	√	◊
b	B	∫	l
n	N	~ (above next "n" typed)	˜
m	M	µ	Â
,	<	≤	¯
.	>	≥	˘
/	?	÷	¿

Index

We'd like to hear your suggestions for improving our indexes. Send email to
index@oreilly.com.

Get even more for your money.

Join the O'Reilly Community, and register the O'Reilly books you own. It's free, and you'll get:

- $4.99 ebook upgrade offer
- 40% upgrade offer on O'Reilly print books
- Membership discounts on books and events
- Free lifetime updates to ebooks and videos
- Multiple ebook formats, DRM FREE
- Participation in the O'Reilly community
- Newsletters
- Account management
- 100% Satisfaction Guarantee

Registering your books is easy:

1. Go to: oreilly.com/go/register
2. Create an O'Reilly login.
3. Provide your address.
4. Register your books.

Note: English-language books only

To order books online:
oreilly.com/store

For questions about products or an order:
orders@oreilly.com

To sign up to get topic-specific email announcements and/or news about upcoming books, conferences, special offers, and new technologies:
elists@oreilly.com

For technical questions about book content:
booktech@oreilly.com

To submit new book proposals to our editors:
proposals@oreilly.com

O'Reilly books are available in multiple DRM-free ebook formats. For more information:
oreilly.com/ebooks

O'REILLY®

Spreading the knowledge of innovators   oreilly.com

The information you need, when and where you need it.

With Safari Books Online, you can:

Access the contents of thousands of technology and business books

- Quickly search over 7000 books and certification guides
- Download whole books or chapters in PDF format, at no extra cost, to print or read on the go
- Copy and paste code
- Save up to 35% on O'Reilly print books
- **New!** Access mobile-friendly books directly from cell phones and mobile devices

Stay up-to-date on emerging topics before the books are published

- Get on-demand access to evolving manuscripts.
- Interact directly with authors of upcoming books

Explore thousands of hours of video on technology and design topics

- Learn from expert video tutorials
- Watch and replay recorded conference sessions

O'REILLY®